THE MAJESTY OF
BIG STEAM

BRIAN SOLOMON

Voyageur
Press

Quarto is the authority on a wide range of topics.

Quarto educates, entertains and enriches the lives of our readers—enthusiasts and lovers of hands-on living.

www.quartoknows.com

First published in 2015 by Voyageur Press, an imprint of Quarto Publishing Group USA Inc., 400 First Avenue North, Suite 400, Minneapolis, MN 55401 USA. Telephone: (612) 344-8100 Fax: (612) 344-8692

quartoknows.com
Visit our blogs at quartoknows.com

Voyageur Press titles are also available at discounts in bulk quantity for industrial or sales-promotional use. For details contact the Special Sales Manager at Quarto Publishing Group USA Inc., 400 First Avenue North, Suite 400, Minneapolis, MN 55401 USA.

10 9 8 7 6 5 4 3 2 1

ISBN: 978-0-7603-4892-5

Acquiring Editor: Todd R. Berger
Project Manager: Caitlin Fultz
Senior Art Director: Brad Springer
Cover Designer: Kent Jensen
Designer: Karl Laun

On the front cover: *Brian Solomon*
On the back cover: *Brian Solomon*
On the frontis: More than two decades after it was retired from regular freight operations, Nickel Plate Road 765 has an opportunity to work as a pusher on the Toledo, Peoria & Western, seen here helping an eastbound freight on May 3, 1980. *Ron Wright*
On the title page: Pennsylvania Railroad M1a 6761 works west of Enola, Pennsylvania, on the Middle Division. *Donald W. Furler*
On the contents page: A titan at work: Union Pacific Big Boy 4002 makes voluminous exhaust leading a freight in central Wyoming. *Robert A. Witbeck*

Printed in China

Dedication

To the memory of John E. Pickett—a good friend and a skilled photographer.

Contents

Acknowledgments

The title *The Majesty of Big Steam* aims to convey awe in the celebration of images of some of the biggest and most powerful steam locomotives to have worked North American rails. In addition, this book chronicles the technological development, application, demise, and reincarnation of these engines.

The text for this book is the culmination of more than two decades of my research and photography. Thanks to my father, Richard Jay Solomon, I've been a student of railroading since early childhood. My early steam interest stems from his photographs of these machines at work; visits to Steamtown at Bellows Falls, Vermont, in the late 1960s and early 1970s; and early impressions of Boston & Maine's Pacific 3713, which was displayed in front of Boston's Museum of Science when I was growing up.

In the 1980s and 1990s, I myself made many trips to photograph big steam in action. In 1991, Southern Pacific's public relations officer, Bob Hoppe, offered me the plum assignment of photographing *Daylight* engine 4449, which was running trips from Redding, California. A few years later, I had the opportunity to speak with many members of the steam fraternity while working for Pentrex Publishing. Then, in 1996, Motorbooks' Lee Klancher contracted me to write *The American Steam Locomotive*, which precipitated my first foray into intensive research on the subject and led to work on many other books on steam locomotives, each advancing my knowledge and understanding of the subject. Thanks to John P. Hankey for history lessons and a better understanding of the Baltimore & Ohio, to Dick Gruber for many introductions within the steam fraternity, and to J. D. Schmid for an appreciation of all things Southern Pacific.

Over the years, my late friend Robert A. Buck tutored me on the finer points of steam locomotives. Bob began watching railroads in the 1930s, and his keen interest in the Boston & Albany is represented in these pages. In addition to guiding my efforts, he introduced me to many knowledgeable steam men and photographers. Many others educated me along the way, including Harry Vallas on the finer points of valve gear; George C. Corey on technical aspects of steam locomotive performance and engine aesthetics; Paul Carver on the particulars of New York Central's engines; Stuart Woolley, a retired Boston & Albany fireman whose colorful tales of the days of steam put life into machines I only knew from photographs; and many others, including members of the West Springfield Train Watchers, a group of enthusiasts, many of whom worked in railroad service during the steam era.

The steam locomotive has inspired a wealth of specialized literature, much of it written in the days when steam power ruled railways around the globe. I've studied the pages of trade journals such as *Baldwin Locomotives*, *Railway & Locomotive Engineering*, *Railway Age*, and *Railway Mechanical Engineer*. I've also read more than my share of books on the subject, including Alfred Bruce's *The Steam Locomotive in America*; George Drury's *Guide to North American Steam Locomotives*; Frank M. Swengel's *The American Steam Locomotive: Volume 1, Evolution*; various books by John H. White Jr., and the extensive writings of former *Trains* magazine editor David P. Morgan. I've included a detailed bibliography of sources in the backmatter.

The power of this book is in the photographs, the work of more than a dozen contributing photographers spanning a century. These images are a tribute to the insight of those men, who tirelessly sought out and photographed steam power across the North American continent. Each of the photographers is credited by their work. Special thanks to Alan Furler for lending me images from his father's collection and to Parsons Witbeck Clark, who allowed me access to her father's wonderful photograph collection. Kenneth and Russell Buck have also lent me photographs from the collection of Robert

A. Buck. John Gruber provided images and text and has made many introductions to steam specialists and photographers over the years.

Thanks to Mark Hemphill and Mel Patrick for help with captioning Rio Grande images. Chris Bost assisted with the captioning of Reading photos. Kurt Bell and Nick Zmijewski of the Railroad Museum of Pennsylvania assisted with photographic research and the history of Baldwin Locomotives. Patrick McKnight aided with research at the Steamtown archives while Paul Hammond aided my research in Baltimore, Sacramento, Minnesota, and Wisconsin on several occasions. In addition, the members of the Irish Railway Record Society allowed me unrestricted access to their extensive library in Dublin.

Pat Yough helped in a great many ways, including organizing trips to visit photographers and to photograph Reading & Northern's 425, the locomotive that appears on the cover of this book. My father also helped by reviewing my text; my mother, Maureen, has assisted with logistics during our family's many railway trips. Thanks finally to Todd R. Berger and everyone at Voyageur Press for bringing this book to completion.

I've made every effort to put big steam in context and to illustrate my text with details of the locomotives. It is my hope that all the information presented here is correct and accurate. However, if errors appear, they are my own and not those of the many people who have guided me.

In the late 1950s, a fireman gazes down the length of the boiler on a Norfolk & Western Y-class Mallet east of Roanoke at Boaz, Virginia. *Jim Shaughnessy*

INTRODUCTION

During the era when the steam locomotive reached its pinnacle, American steam power grew to gigantic proportions—and its largest engines were far larger than any others in the world. With their enormous piston thrusts and incredible pulling power, the massive machines represented the culmination of more than 120 years of continuous research and development. These engines were highly refined and often designed for very specific services, representing the most cost-effective transportation means private industry had during the period.

It would be easy to simply focus on the handful of the very largest locomotives, namely Union Pacific's colossal Big Boy, Chesapeake & Ohio's massive Allegheny, and the impressive Yellowstones that ruled the North Dakota Badlands and the Minnesota Iron Range. These represented the biggest, heaviest, and most powerful reciprocating steam locomotives in the world. Yet, they are only part of the story of big steam. And, owing to the nature of the jobs they were designed to perform, they spent most of their working lives laboring in relative obscurity and largely out of public view. The real story of big steam, both in terms of technological development and in day-to-day service, lies with the many machines that seemed huge to the ordinary person yet were dwarfed by the aforementioned titans of the rails. These pages examine a range of these twentieth-century locomotives, from the everyday Pacifics and Mikados, which represented some of the most common engines, to more specialized giants and some of the rare and obscure machines that once worked North American lines. The illustrations largely present locomotives that were developed in the final 30 years of steam production (roughly from 1920 to 1950) and include a mix of period photos and images from later years that feature revived and preserved engines.

I've included many different locomotives and railroads throughout, profiling and highlighting some of the most significant examples. However, this book is not intended to be a comprehensive listing or a catalog of North American steam power. Rather, it is a celebration of some of the greatest and most impressive locomotives, designed to convey the majesty of the machinery and its applications.

Big Steam

The development of big steam power was a continent-wide movement aimed at obtaining the greatest operating efficiency from the conventional reciprocating steam locomotive. The locomotive attained great proportions not to impress viewers or make spectacular photographic subjects, but rather to keep railroad lines fluid and make the most of infrastructure while handling traffic in the most economical way possible. The size and weight of a specific locomotive design was a function of the specific physical plant (track and related infrastructure) and the job(s) it was intended to perform.

The fundamentals of steam locomotive operation were established early in the 1800s. While the workings of the machines were gradually improved over the years, and the size of individual designs increased (barring the odd exception), most steam locomotives retained the same essential equipment arrangement. Yet while the machines conformed to the basic functional parameters detailed below, their creators' need to work within the limitations of steam locomotive design, combined with various railroads' fiercely individualistic operating cultures, produced significant design variations.

The success of the reciprocating engine and its great reliability and durability made it a fundamental part of railroading for more than a century. To better appreciate the context and significance of the very largest locomotives, and the general role and development of big steam in North America, it is necessary to look at the origins and refinement of the locomotive engine in its formative years.

A Brief Sketch of Early Steam

In eighteenth-century Britain, the steam engine evolved from large single-acting pumping engines. It was famously improved by Scotsman James Watt, who is credited with developing the double-acting reciprocating engine in 1781. Early in the nineteenth century, the steam engine was successfully adapted into a locomotive by Cornishman Richard Trevithick. Both the stationary steam engine and the steam locomotive were chief among innovations that drove the industrial revolution.

Among the most significant early locomotive innovators was George Stephenson, who keenly observed pioneer locomotives built by others (Trevithick, John Blenkinsop, and William Hedley), improved on them, and put them to work. Stephenson not only improved steam locomotive design, but he was the first to combine the locomotive with the pubic railway, which established a precedent mimicked across Britain and around the world. His 12-mile Stockton & Darlington was authorized by an Act of Parliament in 1821 and opened to traffic on September 27, 1825, when Stephenson personally operated his engine, *Locomotion*, leading a train of 34 cars over the railway. This was a step toward Stephenson's ambitious Liverpool & Manchester Railway (L&M), which opened in 1829.

The most significant outcome of the L&M was its famous Rainhill locomotive trials, a competition designed to encourage locomotive development. Four steam locomotives were entered, including Rocket, designed by George's son Robert. Having attained a top speed of 29 mph (extraordinarily fast at that time), Rocket was deemed the hands-down winner. But more significant than its performance at the Rainhill Trials was the design precedents it established. This revolutionary machine rendered all previous designs obsolete and established the design pattern that remained standard for steam locomotive construction for the next 130 years. All the locomotives pictured in this book are descendants of this groundbreaking machine.

Rocket for the first time combined the three principal elements of reciprocating locomotive design: a multitubular (fire-tube) boiler, forced draft from exhaust steam, and direct linkage between the piston and drive wheels. This put an end to clumsy attempts at converting reciprocating motion into rotary motion using rocker arms and arrangements of gears. Soon after Rocket, similar machines were exported to the United States.

North American development resulted in many variations to steam locomotive design that distinguished its engines from those in Britain and elsewhere. By 1900, the proportions and scale of North American engines built for mainline service were remarkably larger than those used elsewhere in the world, and they had just begun their exceptional leap in size and power.

Engines Big and Small

At a casual glance, the tiny wheeled teakettles of the 1820s and 1830s may seem to have little in common with the gigantic machines of the mid-twentieth century. But these early machines were the direct technological ancestors of the later machines that followed and were operated using the same essential principals. The later examples were simply more refined, more efficient, and, of course, larger.

For its time, the steam locomotive offered the best possible economy given the available technology. Ironically, it was the emergence of new technologies, specifically electric and later diesel-electric locomotives, that pushed steam locomotive designs to their ultimate limits. When the diesel-electric was finally proven to offer greater efficiency and lower cost than steam, this new technology rapidly supplanted the old order. Since the 1950s, no large American railroad has seriously considered the steam locomotive for cost-effective transportation. Those steam locomotives that have survived are historical relics, preserved for nostalgia and public enjoyment.

Big Steam

IN THE NINETEENTH CENTURY, when the railroad was the fastest and most efficient means of land transport, the coming of the locomotive was synonymous with progress. The mournful whistle of the locomotive had heralded human connectivity while the nimble 4-4-0 was the most recognizable locomotive type across North America. Even today the silhouette of a classic 4-4-0 American type remains a common icon of railroading, despite more than a century of obsolescence.

Steel and Irony

In the heyday of the old Iron Horse, the 4-4-0 type was universal. However, as railroads sought ever greater efficiency, first to compete with each other and later as a reaction to competition from other transportation modes, improved locomotives were developed to replace older types. In the twentieth century, new materials—specifically commercially produced steel and later improved alloyed steels—joined scientific approaches toward locomotive development, design refinement, and technologies such as superheating to enable new breeds of steam power that were vastly more powerful than the old Iron Horses.

By the 1920s, improved construction techniques, including advances in welding technology and better large-scale casting, helped make stronger engine components while alloyed steel reduced the engine's relative weight. New locomotive designs benefited from higher boiler pressure, more powerful piston thrusts, and significantly lighter reciprocating parts. Advances in valve gear and the application of limited cutoff improved steam admission and thus improved engine efficiency while helping reduce cylinder back pressure (which retarded piston thrust), allowing engines to work faster. Advances to boiler design and the introduction of the four-wheel radial trailing

PREVIOUS PAGE: World War II was still underway when Donald W. Furler exposed this impressive portrait of a westward Lehigh & Hudson River freight (Maybrook, New York, to Port Morris, New Jersey) on October 22, 1944, at Sugar Loaf (one mile west of the Chester, New York, station). *Donald W. Furler*

RIGHT: While the 4-8-4 wheel arrangement was commonly known as the Northern type (following Northern Pacific's pioneering use of the type), Lehigh Valley called its 4-8-4s Wyomings, after the important Pennsylvania coalfields it served. *Donald W. Furler*

OPPOSITE: Santa Fe Mikado No. 3225 leads a northward freight from Belen to Albuquerque, New Mexico, on the afternoon of August 30, 1952. *John E. Pickett*

truck (a key component of Lima's Superpower concept of the mid-1920s) introduced a whole new breed of locomotives capable of supplying large volumes of steam over sustained periods, and this changed the ways that railroads bought and assigned mainline motive power.

In the 1930s, further advancements such as precision counterbalancing, the application of roller-bearings, and significant improvements to articulated locomotive design made it possible to build very large and remarkably fast steam power. But ironically, just as the newer, superheated steel horses were gaining prominence and growing rapidly in size, the railroad transportation mode began to lose its long-held supremacy. Railroads were on the wane, slipping from public consciousness. Furthermore, just as the steam locomotive became most capable, it was replaced by new technology: the diesel electric locomotive.

In 1963, Canadian National shopped 4-8-4 No. 6218, four years after the end of its revenue steam operations. Over the next eight years, this locomotive served as a popular excursion engine, working dozens of trips in the United States and Canada. CN 6218 is photographed here working a Quebec trip in October 1964. *Richard Jay Solomon*

Canadian National 6218 makes a spectacular show of smoke on the approach to a tall tower-supported, steel-girder trestle during a Quebec excursion in October 1964. *Richard Jay Solomon*

Railway enthusiasts drink in the sights and sounds of Reading T-1 2100 leading one of the railroad's enormously popular Iron Horse Rambles in May 1964. *Richard J. Solomon*

Reading Company class T-1 4-8-4 2102 works a Reading & Northern photo-freight at Schuylkill Haven, Pennsylvania, on October 24, 1991. Nostalgia for big steam has seen a number of locomotives returned to service over the last five decades. *Chris Bost*

ABOVE: Reading Company 2102 was only a few years old when this photo captured it leading a 97-car westward freight at Emmaus, Pennsylvania. *Donald W. Furler*

RIGHT: Fireman's side of Milwaukee Road 4-8-4 261 at Galesburg, Illinois. *Brian Solomon*

Overshadowed Locomotive Masterpieces

At the turn of the twentieth century, the railroad was part of the fabric of modern life. Locomotives and trains were the rolling furniture of industrialized society. Then new transportation modes began to capture the public imagination. So while locomotives continuously reached greater degrees of refinement, cresting wave after wave of new power thresholds, they slipped ever farther into the shadows.

Some thoroughbreds—the high-stepping, passenger-hauling masterpieces of engineering like New York Central's Hudsons—continued to catch the public eye. And the introduction of sleek, streamlined steam engines turned a few heads. But public attention is fickle. A fleeting glimpse of the wondrous new steam locomotives was soon overshadowed by a constant and ever-changing modern world.

Pennsylvania Railroad (PRR) placed its mighty S1 Streamlined Duplex on display at the 1939–1940 New York World's Fair, dubbed the World of Tomorrow. But while the elegant Raymond Loewy–styled beast awed the tens of thousands of visitors, General Motors' nearby Magic Motorways exhibition offered another view of the future. After the fair, PRR's S1 labored for a few years in relative obscurity, racing trains across the cornfields of Ohio and Indiana, while the dream of grade-separated superhighways settled in the American consciousness.

During the late 1930s and early 1940s, American railroads took delivery of the most powerful steam locomotives that would ever work the rails on this continent or anywhere else. But despite the occasional appearance in promotional movie newsreels, detailed articles in trade publications, and dramatic photo features in the pages of railway hobby magazines, the greatest steel leviathans were largely out of public view.

The drivers of Milwaukee Road 4-8-4 261 glisten in the evening light at BNSF's Galesburg, Illinois, engine terminal on June 23, 1996. *Brian Solomon*

Unlike the universal 4-4-0 of yesteryear, the modern giants—2-8-8-4 Yellowstones of the Missabe, the 2-6-6-6 Alleghanies on Chesapeake & Ohio, and 4-8-8-4 Big Boys for Union Pacific—toiled in relatively remote regions like the wilds of the Iron Range, the river valleys and mountain summits of Appalachia, and the high plains and wide-open spaces of central Wyoming. Most people never saw one of these monsters at work. Perhaps as you rode west on the *City of San Francisco* you might catch a glimpse of one of the mighty 4000s with its 24 wheels as it blasted by with a mile of refrigerated boxcars, but then again you might have missed it. This is a shame, for they were among the most impressive machines on Earth.

Less Was More

The relative numbers of locomotives on the move diminished as individual engine types became more powerful and more efficient. But that was the whole idea: to put more power in the hands of the individual locomotive engineer and allow the engine crew to do more work. So the more efficient use of locomotives—longer runs, more reliable machinery, and better maintenance—resulted in railroad companies requiring far fewer locomotives to move trains. Consequently most of the more modern monsters were built in relatively limited numbers.

Another contributing factor was the relatively long life inherent in steam locomotive design. Provided it was maintained and rebuilt every few years, an individual engine could last for decades. Many locomotives built in 1910 were still at work in 1950. So while improved designs reduced the numbers of locomotives required on the heaviest and fastest trains, much of the menial work continued to be performed by older engines.

OPPOSITE: The massive 4-8-8-4 Big Boy leading this mile-long freight looks like a mere speck on the horizon coughing a wisp of dark smoke. *Jim Shaughnessy*

TOP: At 10:30 a.m. on July 30, 1988, former Nickel Plate Road 2-8-4 Berkshire 765 works an excursion on the former Erie Railroad mainline at Tuxedo, New York. *George W. Kowanski*

BOTTOM: One of Nickel Plate Road's high-driver 2-8-4 Berkshires marches east at speed near Westfield, New York, in the mid-1950s. *Jim Shaughnessy*

NEXT PAGE: Erie Railroad 3384, one of its class S-3 2-8-4 Berkshires, leads a westward freight with 99 cars at Allendale, New Jersey, in the 1940s. *Donald W. Furler*

Perception versus Reality

The postwar motorist in his new car took note when he paused at a rural grade crossing and a 600,000-pound mass of steel with more than 100 freight cars in tow flashed in front of him. That wasn't the locomotive of his grandfather's day! He might have wondered for a moment how "the little engine that could" had become so big.

The majesty of steam power was also a reflection on the inherent inefficiencies of the reciprocating locomotive engine. While for more than a century it had offered the best solution for the mass transportation of goods and people by rail, the steam engine's fundamental design limitations ultimately sealed its doom.

In the eyes of the steam enthusiast, the relatively rapid demise of American steam after a century of continuous refinement was a technological tragedy. The finest steam locomotives ever built had short service lives. New York Central's thoroughbred Hudsons worked for a little more than 15 years and its supremely refined 4-8-4 Niagara for fewer than 10. What's more, railroads such as Central, which continued to order steam after World War II, were in the minority. Yet most postwar steam was built to some of the most highly refined designs, such as Lima's high-driver Berkshires for Nickel Plate Road and powerful 4-8-4s for Chesapeake & Ohio.

A few lines looking to stave off dieselization bought well-built but obsolete types. Rutland bought four Alco 4-8-2 Mountains in 1946, only to come back to Alco for more versatile diesel road switchers a few years later. Baltimore & Ohio, although among the early proponents of diesel power, kept its shop forces busy for a few years after World War II by building 4-8-2s. The last of these was finished in 1948, at a time when several major railroads were approaching total dieselization.

Norfolk & Western (N&W) was a special case. It was among the lines closely wedded to bituminous coal traffic, and therefore found the promise of dieselization unappetizing. Because it both designed and built most of its own locomotives and enjoyed abundant coal resources along its lines, it had different priorities than most other railroads. So N&W continued to design, build, and operate mainline steam longer than any other major railroad in the United States.

ABOVE: Boston & Maine R-1 4-8-2 leads symbol freight MB-1 eastbound near West Concord, Massachusetts, on December 7, 1941. At the time, neither the photographer nor the train crew knew the world was about to change. *George C. Corey*

OPPOSITE: On August 25, 1940, Boston & Maine's short-lived East Wind prepares to depart Maine's Portland Union Station for Washington, DC, behind B&M R-1 Mountain 4104. *George C. Corey*

LEFT: Chesapeake & Ohio 4-8-4 614 leads an excursion on the old Erie Railroad seen crossing the Ramapo River near Tuxedo, New York, on October 20, 1996. *G. W. Kowanski*

BELOW LEFT: Baker valve gear arrangement on Chesapeake & Ohio 4-8-4 No. 614, photographed at Port Jervis, New York. *Brian Solomon*

N&W's final J-Class 4-8-4s of 1950 were the last new North American passenger steam engines and the final example of this wheel arrangement in the United States. Its articulated types represented some of the most refined heavy road power on the continent, of which its final Y6B (built in 1952) was the last of heavy reciprocating steam for road service. In 1953, it outshopped a final batch of 0-8-0s. In 1954, it made one final foray into steam development by ordering an experimental steam-turbine-electric from Baldwin-Westinghouse. This couldn't match the operating costs of General Motors' road switchers, and it was retired in 1957, three years before N&W's final mainline steam operations in 1960.

On the evening of August 25, 1956, locomotive designs spanning five decades sit side by side at the St. Luc engine terminal in Montreal. *Jim Shaughnessy*

RIGHT: The drivers on a Canadian National Railways 4-8-4 at Dorval, Quebec, made for an impressive sight. *Jim Shaughnessy*

ABOVE: Canadian National Railways 4-6-2 Pacific 5280 leads a short passenger train at Dorval, Quebec, on November 11, 1957. *Jim Shaughnessy*

LEFT: Canadian National Railway class U-1f 4-8-2 6060 leads a passenger excursion at Murray Bay, Quebec, on September 26, 1976. *George W. Kowanski*

Delaware, Lackawanna & Western's three-cylinder Mountain type 2227 leads an eastbound extra freight at Blairstown, New Jersey. *Donald W. Furler*

Mysteries of Modern Steam

The term *modern steam* may seem like an oxymoron. How could a machine that owed its lineage to the geriatric contraptions of the previous century be deemed modern? But late-era steam wasn't just big; it was more efficient and more complicated than the old engines of the mid-nineteenth century.

The 4-4-0 enjoyed a simple straightforward design with little complexity. Its operation and function were relatively easy to comprehend from a visual study of the equipment. By the 1920s, locomotives had embraced a host of innovations, ranging from superheating elements and feedwater heaters to thermic siphons, automatic stokers, booster engines, and sophisticated lubrication and sanding systems. The result was that the workings of the steam locomotive had been significantly improved, yet the means of operation for these improvements tended to be hidden from the casual observer. Spotting an Elesco feedwater heater hanging on the smokebox of a modern engine only showed the locomotive was so equipped; it gave little indication as to how the equipment actually worked.

The cab of a nineteenth-century locomotive had relative few appurtenances—a throttle to regulate the flow of steam to the cylinders, a Johnson bar to adjust the valves and control the direction and power of the engine, an engine brake, whistle and bell cords, firebox doors, a water sight to monitor the level of water in the boiler, and injector controls to fill it. By contrast, by the 1920s a locomotive cab was filled with an intimidating array of knobs, levers, valves, sights, and alarms used to operate the host of appliances necessary to make the locomotive work.

Textbooks on locomotive design filled thousands of pages, and the engineering details for an individual machine required hundreds of blueprints. While the most basic operation of the engine remained rooted in Robert Stephenson's Rocket of 1829, a century of improvements shrouded the locomotive in complex equipment, including a host of auxiliary appliances, many of which were offered to locomotive builders by third-party suppliers.

Thunder on the Mountain

One man's problem is another man's opportunity. Such was the case in steam railroading. The laws of physics constrain railroad operation over mountain grades. The limitations of adhesion (friction) between wheel and rail was (and remains) a great complication to railroad operation. In steam railroading the most dramatic applications of power were on heavy grades, where the largest locomotives would labor fore and aft under clouds of their own exhaust on tonnage trains. But while graded operation was the perpetual thorn in the side of the operating department, the thunder on the mountain thrilled onlookers, and skilled photographers sought out the most difficult operations to make their most dramatic images of engines at work.

The earliest railroad builders in nineteenth-century Britain didn't understand adhesion, so there was a popular misconception that iron wheels on iron rails would slip uncontrollably on a grade. As a result many early railways were built with low-grade, "water-level" profiles.

In America this philosophy resulted in excessively sinuous routes, where lines curved to avoid climbing wherever possible. The construction of inclined planes was a compromise for extremely steep ascents where trains were hauled with cables powered by stationary engines. Pennsylvania's famed "Main Line of Public Works," which linked Philadelphia and Pittsburgh through a network of canals and railways, was one of the most extreme applications of inclined planes.

While low-grade construction was possible on a large scale in Britain, American engineers faced far more difficult terrain and smaller construction budgets. By the late 1830s, American engineers were aiming to construct mountain railroads, previously deemed impossible by naysayers, canal proponents, and others. In the 1830s, George Washington Whistler surveyed a route west from Worcester, Massachusetts, toward Albany, New York. Massachusetts's Western Rail Road, the state-sponsored extension of the key Boston & Worcester line, faced a succession of grades, the steepest considered at the time without the aid of inclined planes.

Whistler engineered his line to high standards. He wasn't content with the slipshod construction characteristics of some of the early American railways, instead insisting on the best possible grade by using cuts and fills. Immediately after leaving Worcester, Whistler's line climbed over the relatively steep Charlton Summit and reached the wide Connecticut River at Springfield, Massachusetts, in 1839. But the most difficult section of the railroad to build and operate was its eastern ascent of the Berkshires, where Whistler engineered a sinuous 1.67

Canadian Pacific 2317 was among the star performers at the Steamtown National Historic Site based in Scranton, Pennsylvania. On September 14, 1991, it leads an excursion working toward Moscow, Pennsylvania.
George W. Kowanski

percent grade (meaning a climb of 1.67 feet for every 100 traveled) that required a series of large stone arch bridges and deep rock cuts excavated with black powder and steam shovels.

In 1867, Western and B&W merged to become the Boston & Albany, and in 1900 this was leased by New York Central System. Whistler's railway was so well engineered that most of his original alignment survives on the present CSX mainline in New England. Only a few short segments were relocated in the steam era. Yet, since the Berkshire grade opened to traffic in

1841, it has required special breeds of motive power. Whistler attempted to solve the problem of graded operation by ordering a novel fleet of the world's first eight-coupled locomotives from his friend Ross Winans of Baltimore.

Winans's 0-8-0 was designed with small wheels to deliver high tractive effort at slow speeds while distributing the weight over four axles. The engines were enormous for their day, weighing in at 22½ tons. By any measure, these were strange machines. Unlike most of the later American locomotives,

ABOVE: This view shows the pushers at the back of the same freight led by Delaware & Hudson Challenger 1534.
Donald W. Furler

LEFT: In a stupendous show of power, Delaware & Hudson Challenger 1534 leads northward symbol freight WM-3 at Carbondale, Pennsylvania. Three sets of locomotives were working at the back. *Donald W. Furler*

these were not descendants of Stephenson's Rocket and didn't resemble typical steam locomotives. Instead the design had its origins in machines derived from marine practice by Phineas Davis and Peter Cooper. Seven were built in total, and eventually became known colloquially as "mud diggers" and "crabs" because of their peculiar motion. They were not successful, but they demonstrated the special requirements for locomotives in graded territory.

In the 1920s, Boston & Albany's Berkshire grades were the proving ground for Lima's first Superpower, an extraordinary locomotive concept that began with the 2-8-4 wheel arrangement. In honor of the grade, the 2-8-4 was coined the Berkshire type (featured in Chapter 3).

BELOW: Erie 4102, an R-2 class 2-10-2, leads an empty hopper train westward across the Mill Rift Bridge over the Delaware River west of Port Jervis, New York. *Donald W. Furler*

How Big Was Big Steam?

The story of the steam locomotive is something like the proverbial fishing story of the one that got away: as the story progresses, the subject grows to a preposterous size. Except in the case of the locomotive it really was *that* big.

The handful of truly gargantuan machines built in the final years of steam power only tells the penultimate chapter in the story of big steam. While the very largest examples of steam power were conceived in the last decade or so of development in late 1930s and 1940s, the story of big steam goes back decades earlier.

In his 1907 book, *Development of the Locomotive Engine*, author Angus Sinclair reflects on the American locomotive engine and the details of its history up to that point: "The primary goal of the locomotive designer from the beginning was to produce a simple, dependable, powerful machine." The undertone of Sinclair's analysis is a lament of the large proportions that locomotives had reached at that time and the fact that the more conservatively sized engines of the previous century were being completely eclipsed by the new order. "The world has frequently seen the village church expand into an imposing cathedral," he notes. He further elaborates, saying, "The trend of locomotive building in 1907 is toward enormously heavy engines, large Consolidation becoming common on perfectly level railroads. For operating mountain railroads the Mallet articulated double-ended compound . . . is into favor." If Sinclair felt the heavy consolidations and early Mallet types of 1907 were too large, we can only imagine what he might have felt at the prospect of a 4-6-6-4 Challenger racing along at 70 mph, let alone the sight of the Challenger's big brother, the legendary 4-8-8-4 Big Boy, which produced more than 7,000 horsepower.

More than six decades after *Development of the Locomotive Engine*'s original release, locomotive historian John H. White Jr. produced an annotated edition of Sinclair's history in which he aimed to correct some of the minor technical inaccuracies of the original work without interrupting its narrative and bring the book up to date. White's own research and writing fills the final pages, offering a succinct, insightful review of American steam development in the era of big steam. White identifies the year 1890 as "the point of departure" in locomotive design. He notes that up until the 1890s, American locomotives were generally equal in size and power to locomotives throughout the world. Weight is a good measure of size, and in the 1890s typical locomotives weighed between 60 and 90 tons. But by the end of the big steam era, American locomotives had reached more than 400 tons.

Locomotives of the late nineteenth century were largely 4-4-0 Americans, 2-6-0 Moguls, 4-6-0 Ten Wheelers, and 2-8-0 Consolidations. Among the most important advancements that precipitated rapid locomotive growth was the introduction of the radial trailing truck. Alfred Bruce writes in his book *The Steam Locomotive in America* that this development "permitted the firebox to be placed entirely behind the drivers and over the trailing truck." Overcoming limitations to firebox size enabled the construction of much larger boilers and resulted in the rapid introduction of new locomotive types and the corresponding swell in the size of new engines. During the first decade of the twentieth century, the 4-4-2 Atlantic, 4-6-2 Pacific, and 2-8-2 Mikado became common designs, while the 1904 introduction of the Mallet type to America opened up a whole new avenue for large locomotive development.

Another key gauge of size is the locomotive's boiler and its contribution to total power output. Frank M. Swengel's detailed work *The American Steam Locomotive: Volume*

1—Evolution carefully chronicles the growth of locomotives. During the early twentieth century, when locomotives entered the era of big steam power, output increased rapidly. The run-up to World War I was an especially important era in locomotive growth. As Swengel writes, "Horsepower capabilities of the typical non-articulated locomotive had jumped from about 1,000 in 1900, up to 1,500 in 1906, and had continued the upward spiral until 2,500 to 3,000 horsepower was a common value by 1916." The most common types of this era were large 2-8-0 Consolidations and 2-8-2 Mikados for general freight work, with 4-6-2s built in large numbers for mainline passenger service.

On October 25, 1959, Reading operated the first of its popular Iron Horse Rambles with T1 No. 2124. The popular locomotive was surrounded by thrilled fans a few weeks later on its November 14, 1959, trip to Valley Forge, Pennsylvania. *Richard J. Solomon*

In the early 1950s, Union Pacific 4-12-2 9016 starts a heavy freight. This enormous variety of locomotive was unique to the railroad and known as the Union Pacific type. *Robert A. Witbeck*

Swengel goes on to note, "The other great and noticeable characteristic of motive power in 1916, was that no two railroads agreed on design, proportions or features of their newest motive power." And railroads that couldn't find common ground in regard to nonarticulated design couldn't be expected to take restrained approaches in the development of the larger articulated types. During the second decade of the twentieth century, several railroads ordered some bizarrely proportioned articulated locomotives, using what might be considered freakish wheel arrangements in their disparate efforts to push the limits of power and design.

Santa Fe briefly followed a peculiar developmental path. While many railroads of the time had adopted Mallet compounds with small drivers for low-speed, heavy-freight service, beginning in 1909, Santa Fe encouraged Mallet development as high-speed passenger locomotives with tall drivers. It experimented with different wheel arrangements, including two locomotives that employed an unorthodox 4-4-6-2 arrangement. A number of its high-speed Mallets were built with jointed boilers for greater flexibility. Meanwhile, in 1911, Santa Fe used components from 2-10-2s to build 10 massive 2-10-10-2 Mallets for slow-speed freight service; these monsters were briefly the world's largest locomotives. Like many radical departures from conventional practice, the costs associated with operating these peculiar types outweighed any performance improvements. Consequently, most of Santa Fe's Mallets had very short service lives. The 2-10-10-2s were eventually rebuilt as conventional locomotives.

Despite these setbacks, Santa Fe briefly entertained even more bizarre engines in the form of a cab-forward, oil-burning "quadruplex" (2-8-8-8-8-2) and even "quintuplex" (2-8-8-8-8-8-2) steam locomotive types. Although drawings for such outlandish machines exist, none were constructed. Yet the concept of putting four and five power units under the control of one crew wasn't forgotten. As impractical as it was for a steam locomotive to be built in this manner, Santa Fe would eventually be the first to order Electro-Motive's model FT 4-unit (A-B-B-A) diesel-electrics in 1940.

The majority of American steam locomotives never approached the most extreme sizes, but the average locomotive of 1929 was vastly larger than its forebears of 30 years

On March 18, 1961, National Railways of Mexico's 4-8-4 Niagara 3050 leads a northward freight of American railroad boxcars north of Mexico City. *Jim Shaughnessy*

earlier. The most extreme examples of American steam were built to fulfill atypical situations. Northern Pacific's 2-8-8-4 Yellowstones, built in the late 1920s with vast fireboxes, were designed to eliminate double heading in the difficult district east of Glendive, Montana, while taking advantage of locally mined low-yield coal. If Northern Pacific had had easy access to better fuel, would these engines have been quite so large?

Other late-era monsters, such as Union Pacific's Big Boy and Pennsylvania's divided-drive Duplex types, were innovative reactions to the debut of the diesel-electric, which was threatening to undermine steam. Traditional steam designers wanted to demonstrate they could match and exceed the output of early road diesels. While the machines were certainly impressive to see in action, time would show that the accountants weren't impressed—raw output was only part of the equation.

This situation raises a variety of hypothetical scenarios. What if locomotive builders had developed reliable road diesels a decade or two sooner? What if adequate financing had been available for electrification after World War I, and mainline railroads had invested in large-scale heavy mainline electrification similar to what was demonstrated by New Haven Railroad and Milwaukee Road? What if Archduke Franz Ferdinand had stayed in Vienna and World War I never happened? What if the railroads had played a more sophisticated political game in the early twentieth century and prevented the draconian and misguided antitrust legislation that made it difficult for them to make massive infrastructure investment in the first place? If history had followed a different path, then the massive late-era steam locomotives might never have been built. Or, perhaps, even bigger engines would have ruled the rails. It is impossible to know.

Six-Coupled: Pacifics and Hudsons

AT THE DAWN OF THE TWENTIETH CENTURY, when the world's largest locomotives labored in obscurity—massive 2-10-2s worked as helpers on Colorado's Raton Pass—the 4-6-2 Pacific emerged front and center. As it grew in popularity, it became the locomotive that you saw passing through small-town America with the famous limited in tow.

It was this locomotive that brought your father to work, or that you rode behind when taking your first big railway trip. It was a Pacific you saw simmering under the shed at South Station in Boston with the *New York Express* bound for Albany or leading the luxurious *Merchants Limited* destined for New York City. It was the type of locomotive hauling the *Lackawanna Limited*

from Hoboken Terminal and nearby on the *Erie Limited* at Jersey City. It was a Pacific under the shed at Chicago & North Western station with your transcontinental sleeping car train, and when the train arrived at the Oakland Mole on San Francisco Bay, there was another Pacific, this one operated by Southern Pacific. It was probably a Pacific's exhaust and clatter

over jointed trail that blues musicians of the Mississippi Delta sang of in their songs. Today, if you visit the Smithsonian in Washington, DC, it is a Southern Railway Pacific you will see on display—the representative of big steam.

Development of the Pacific

The Pacific type—defined by its 4-6-2 wheel arrangement—was the locomotive type that seemed to epitomize the transition to big steam in the early years of the twentieth century. It also had one of the longest production runs of any twentieth-century type. While it was neither the most numerous nor by any means the largest locomotive, as the preferred passenger type from the early years of the century until the Great Depression, it was the locomotive type most familiar to the public—it was the face of the American railroad.

If you had visited just about any major railway station during the first half of the twentieth century, from Portland, Maine, to San Diego, California, from Quebec City to Mexico City, you probably would have found Pacifics leading all varieties of passenger trains from the company's leading flagship to the all-stops suburban local. More than 6,000 of the type were built between 1902 and 1948, and while the Pacific lost its superiority to larger types in its last 20 years of production, on a great many lines Pacifics survived in daily traffic until diesels took over in the 1950s.

The earliest applications of the 4-6-2 wheel arrangement have been subject to intricate pedantic analysis, as this wheel arrangement was variously tried for both domestic and export use in the last decade of the nineteenth century. Yet these early examples did not have noteworthy influences on later development. By contrast, the development and application of the 4-6-2 as America's premier twentieth-century passenger steam locomotive is an easier story to follow, and the primary focus here.

OPPOSITE: Bessemer & Lake Erie 4-6-2 901 simmers at the Erie, Pennsylvania, engine facility in 1949. *J. William Vigrass*

In a thrilling display of smoke and steam, Canadian Pacific 4-6-2 2203 and Mikado 5187 double head a train at Campbellville, Ontario, near Guelph Junction on August 1, 1957. *Jim Shaughnessy*

STRIVING FOR LARGER, FASTER PASSENGER POWER

The emergence of the 4-6-2 as a powerful passenger engine was the culmination of locomotive trends that had pushed the envelope of steam design in the late nineteenth century. The Pacific, like most new reciprocating steam locomotives, was the result of combining evolutionary improvements rather than the application of revolutionary new technology. Except for the novel wheel arrangement, there was virtually nothing employed on early Pacifics that hadn't been previously tried on earlier types.

When it was new, railroads considered the Pacific type to be a big passenger locomotive. Its adoption was made possible by gradual improvements to American railroad infrastructure. These advancements permitted significant increases to locomotive maximum axle weight and clearance improvements to allow for larger boilers, including heavier rail, better engineered rights of way, larger clearances, and much stronger bridges.

As previously discussed, in the last decades of the nineteenth century, both the maximum locomotive size and typical locomotive size grew dramatically. In the 1870s, locomotives weighing 50 tons were typical, but by 1900 locomotives weighing 110 tons were being built, and engines kept getting bigger every year.

The innovation of the radial load-bearing trailing truck changed the way locomotive builders thought about firebox and boiler design. The addition of a trailing truck at the back of the engine helped support a portion of the firebox while freeing it from the confines of the locomotive frames. This change allowed for a much larger and deeper firebox than previously possible (because trailing truck wheels were significantly lower than drivers). It also made it possible to build a locomotive with a substantially larger boiler with greater steam capacity. The trailing truck also increased stability and provided better ride quality.

Metallurgical advances were another significant change, yet more difficult for the casual observer to appreciate. It was easy enough to see how heavier rail and new, more robust bridges would allow for construction of larger locomotives, and how the radial trailing truck liberated locomotive design from the historical constraints of the locomotive frame on firebox size. By comparison, the blending of steel alloys to make stronger and lighter grades of steel was practically invisible. However, improved steel enabled locomotive designers to build larger and better boilers that could operate with significantly higher pressure. In short, incremental design changes during the 1890s allowed for the rapid evolution of new locomotive wheel arrangements.

One of the most influential of the new locomotives made its debut at the Columbian Exposition in Chicago in 1893. This was a Baldwin-built Vauclain compound, a patented four-cylinder compound design where pairs of high- and low-pressure cylinders were located on each side of the locomotive in a side-by-side arrangement and connected to a common cross head. This elegant machine, designed to demonstrate the potential of a new wheel arrangement, was named Columbia to mark the significance of the event. Swengel noted that it was "beautifully finished, painted and polished in every detail, and her machined surfaces polished and gleaming." The 2-4-2 arrangement defined the Columbia type. The pioneer machine featured abnormally tall drivers—just over 7 feet in diameter—while its leading pony truck also had unusually large wheels. And of course it had the significant firebox trailing truck that would prove to be the type's most lasting development.

Although Columbia wasn't the first locomotive to employ pony wheels below the firebox, its high-profile application demonstrated the value of the design, setting a precedent advanced by Baldwin on subsequent locomotive types. The 2-4-2 wheel arrangement was not widely adopted, but its trailing truck led to the introduction of the 4-4-2 Atlantic and 2-6-2 Prairie, both of which enjoyed enormous success over the next dozen years.

The 4-6-2 wheel arrangement was the next logical step and blended the best characteristics of the 4-6-0, 2-6-2, and 4-4-2 types while overcoming the principal limitations of each of those designs. The 4-6-2 enjoyed excellent front-end stability and had a large boiler for ample sustained steam capacity for both power and speed, as well as high drivers for fast running.

RIGHT: Boston & Albany
Pacific 526 leads the
westbound *Wolverine* near
Wellesley, Massachusetts.
*F. H. Worcester, collection of
Robert A. Buck*

A NEED FOR SPEED

By the 1890s, several American railroads were operating relatively fast trains. New York Central was among the lines that operated famously fast expresses. In 1893, it demonstrated unprecedented speed with its famed 999, a specially built 4-4-0 with exceptionally tall drivers that made a one-of-a-kind press run on May 10 of that year. Working west from Batavia, New York, with a press run of the *Empire State Express*, it was reported to have briefly hit 112.5 mph. While the accuracy of this speed record has been questioned, there's little doubt that the engine ran exceptionally fast that day. More to the point, it established New York Central's *Empire State Express* as a really fast train.

Where on normal days in the 1890s New York Central's top express trains might hit the high two digits, the motive power options for the trains posed a problem. The old standard 4-4-0 American type had just about reached the limit of its development. The 4-4-2 was built as a fast engine, but like the 4-4-0 it was limited in its ability to haul long trains. The 4-6-0 type made for a better heavy passenger engine but wasn't well suited to high-speed running. For a few years the 2-6-2 Prairie seemed like the answer, and Central's Lake Shore & Michigan Southern was among the railroads that bought this type for fast service. However the 2-6-2 tended to be unstable at high speeds.

The Pacific offered ample boiler capacity, great stability, and excellent tractive effort. It could start a heavy train, get it up to speed relatively quickly, and maintain sustained fast running without running out of steam. This made the type desirable both to railroads with relatively level line-profiles, like New York Central, and those facing prolonged grades.

The key to this new type was the use of a radial trailing truck to produce a 4-6-2 arrangement. This allowed for

a big boiler, which could supply enough steam for sustained high speed; as the type matured, locomotives were designed with ever bigger and more efficient boilers. Swengel explains the importance of ample boiler capacity for fast running: "Almost any boiler would supply steam to the cylinders at very low speed, since the total weight of steam, even at full admission [valves opened to their maximum setting] was limited by the cylinder displacement at low piston speeds. Only as speeds built up, did the demand for steam tend to increase to the point where the boiler capacity limited the output of the locomotive."

EARLY PACIFICS

Although eastern roads such as New York Central, Pennsylvania, and Reading had tended to advance locomotive development, the first domestic order for the 4-6-2 was the Missouri Pacific from American Locomotive Company's Brooks Works in 1902. American Locomotive Company, better known as Alco, had only been formed a year earlier in June of 1901 as the result of the consolidation of a

On August 1, 1952, venerable New York Central System Pacific-type 4461 whisks a train of empty passenger cars along the Harlem Division near Purdy, New York. *Donald W. Furler*

number of smaller locomotive manufacturers, including the Brooks Locomotive Works at Dunkirk, New York, and the Schenectady Locomotive Works of its New York namesake. Over the next four decades, Alco would prove to be one of the leading innovators in American steam design and become the second-largest commercial builder after Philadelphia's Baldwin Locomotive Company. The 4-6-2 type was among Alco's earliest innovations.

Swengel writes, "the name 'Pacific' type, was a tribute to [those] who pioneered the type in America" (i.e., the Missouri Pacific). While this is consistent with many other type names, it has also been suggested that "Pacific" may come from an export order for New Zealand that predated any domestic application. Not withstanding the origin, the 4-6-2 was universally known as the Pacific type, and it was among the few instances where the name carried over to England and other countries. Perhaps the romantic imagery conveyed by the name contributed to its universal acceptance; we may speculate that if it were the Missouri type, it might not have been as widely adopted.

At the time of the construction of Missouri Pacific's engines, the 4-6-2 arrangement was known by another name, as reported in the pages of *Railway & Locomotive Engineering* in August 1902 in an article titled "New Passenger Engines for Missouri Pacific": "Some years ago an engine with this wheel arrangement was built for the Chicago, Milwaukee & St. Paul road, and one of the technical papers subsequently described it as the 'St Paul' type for that reason."

George Drury notes these early examples in his *Guide to North American Steam Locomotives*, dating the first to 1887 and three additional machines built in 1893, along with an even earlier 4-6-2 built for Lehigh Valley. However, while these engines carried a trailing axle, they didn't feature the defining radial trailing truck, and as a result may be regarded as experimental curiosities rather than a step toward later development.

In addition to the new wheel arrangement, Missouri Pacific's engines mark the changes in construction indicative of the early twentieth century and the departure from earlier practices. The "New Passenger Engines for Missouri Pacific" article highlights some notable features: "The Missouri Pacific locomotive has steel castings used in its construction wherever it is desirable to reduce weight. The driving wheels and the carrying truck are all equalized; steel equalizer castings pivoted upon circular pins are used throughout. The spring hangers have top joints made of steel castings of hook-shaped section, with side webs. They grasp a slightly raised knob on the ends of the springs. This makes a strong though flexible form of construction." Also noted was its use of cylindrical piston valves, which were novel at the time but would soon become standard equipment on most new locomotives, replacing the older style of slide valves.

Soon after Missouri Pacific's order, Chesapeake & Ohio bought 4-6-2s with nearly identical characteristics. More

railroads were soon to follow, and as early as 1903, the type was becoming widely accepted as a mainline passenger locomotive. By 1907, the 4-6-2 dominated orders for passenger locomotives.

As might be expected, New York Central was quick to adopt the Pacific to take advantage of its power and speed potential. Alco's Schenectady Works constructed Central's first five Pacifics in 1903, and these featured the pioneer application of Alco's Cole trailing truck. This equipment was designed by one of the company's most influential engineers, Francis J. Cole, who made several key contributions to Pacific design and whom author John H. White Jr. cites as among the most influential locomotive designers of the early twentieth century. Another significant attribute to Central's early Pacific design was its pioneering use of cast-steel main frames. In May 1904, *Railway and Locomotive Engineering* wrote that this offered "strong lateral bracing."

The Pacific was a transitional locomotive type that spanned key design advances. Early Pacifics, such as those described above, used a short-lived valve arrangement with modern piston valves and the older inside valve gear of the Stephenson type, resulting in an unusual off-center arrangement so the valves could be connected inside. This seems odd when compared with more modern engines, where the cylindrical valves were located directly on top of the cylinders (a change facilitated by the introduction of outside valve gear after 1904). Other significant improvements included the introduction of superheating, which resulted in overall improvement to the locomotive's efficiency.

The type emerged at precisely the right time to be useful as a heavy passenger locomotive, and its rapid and sustained popularity paralleled the equally fast growth in the weight of passenger trains and the greater demand for faster schedules.

By comparison, the 4-4-2 Atlantic, which had demonstrated great speed potential, proved ill suited to hauling the long consists that became more common in the early twentieth century.

Not only had passenger trains grown longer as a result of rapidly rising ridership before World War I, but train consists were now more likely to include dining cars as well as "head-end" (mail and express package) traffic. The gradual switch from wooden equipment during the first two decades of the century, first to steel-framed cars and finally to all-steel cars, also contributed to heavier consists. American railroads began phasing out wooden equipment as the result of horrific disasters that had demonstrated the dangers of wooden car bodies. Not only were they susceptible to fire, but they tended to "telescope" (one car body sliding over another) when trains crashed at speed or collided with one another. Pennsylvania Railroad was an early proponent of steel cars.

In a classic scene, three Pennsylvania Railroad class K4s Pacifics charge upgrade at the famous Horseshoe Curve west of Altoona, Pennsylvania.
Robert A. Witbeck

Pennsylvania K4s Pacific 3751 leads a New York & Long Branch run along Raritan Bay beyond the end electrification at South Amboy, circa 1954.
Donald W. Furler

BIG PACIFICS

In the second decade of the twentieth century, the advent of superheating helped satisfy the ever-growing demand for power. The superheater, a European innovation, was introduced into American practice beginning about 1910; thereafter, it was widely adopted on most new locomotive designs. A superheater is an arrangement of tubes and pipes that recirculates boiler steam through tubes in enlarged boiler flues, raising steam temperature by at least 200 degrees Fahrenheit before being admitted to the cylinders for expansion to drive the engine. Superheated steam stores more heat energy for a given volume, thereby increasing its expansive power in the cylinders.

Further design improvements produced some impressively larger Pacifics with very wide boilers offering greater power. This change resulted in many railroads distinguishing between the older "light" Pacifics and the newer "heavy" Pacific engines. Where the early Pacifics weighed 87–130 tons, later heavy Pacifics weighed upward of 150 tons.

Boston & Maine P4 Pacific
3711 leads train 52 at
Concord, Massachusetts,
in December 1945.
George C. Corey

Alco continued to innovate; in 1911, it built a "super" Pacific, assigned number 50,000 to reflect the 50,000th locomotive built by Alco's various component works. This demonstration locomotive, intended to forward modern design, influenced the Pennsylvania Railroad's standard Pacific design, which reached a new plateau in 1914. That year, the railroad introduced the K4s class Pacific (the small *s* stood for "superheated"), an engine widely held as one of finest examples of the type and among the most perfect American locomotives.

PRR was among the railroads that designed large Pacifics in parallel with state-of-the-art 2-8-2 Mikados. In July 1914, *Railway & Locomotive Engineering* offered this insight into the company's locomotive philosophy: "During the last few years the Pennsylvania Railroad Company has felt the need of a larger freight locomotive for use on the main line between Altoona and Pittsburgh, in order to reduce double-heading to a minimum and avoid breaking up trains at Altoona and Pittsburgh before sending them forward over the Pittsburgh Division. It

This view at South Acton in August 1949 finds Boston & Maine Pacific 3712 leading train 5507, which handled empty milk cars to Bellows Falls, Vermont. *George C. Corey*

On March 24, 1946, engineer William "Smitty" Smith is at the throttle of Erie K5A Pacific 2936 leading train 1, the westward *Erie Limited* at Howells, New York. *Donald W. Furler*

was also thought desirable to experiment with a very heavy Pacific type for passenger service on this same division."

The L1s Mikado and K4s Pacific were thus designed in tandem, and both benefited from PRR's scientific approach, which involved using the Altoona test plant to optimize equipment. These engine designs shared many common components and, notably, used the same boiler. The principal difference was in the running gear. The first L1s 2-8-2 was ready in May 1914, and the first K4s 4-6-2 a month later.

PRR continued to order new K4s Pacifics for the next 13 years; many of these machines were built by the company's Juniata Shops in Altoona. Ultimately, it employed 425 of the type among more than 650 4-6-2s in all, which represented more than 10 percent of the total North American Pacific production. Although originally hand-fired, the K4s boiler could consume up to 4½ tons of coal an hour. That's a lot of coal to shovel, and it could break the back of the fireman unless he was exceptionally fit. Ultimately, PRR began equipping its big Pacifics with automatic stokers.

Some K4s Pacifics remained in service until the end of PRR's steam era in 1957. Two were preserved, and for many years one made for a popular display at the famed Horseshoe Curve west of Altoona.

After World War I, Erie Railroad adapted a design for a heavy Pacific, Class K-5, from the United States Railroad Administration (see Chapter 3). The railroad placed several orders for engines with large-diameter boilers for use on its long-distance trains between its Jersey City terminal (on the west shore of the Hudson opposite Manhattan) and Chicago. These engines were significantly larger than its pre–World War I 4-6-2s and gave the railroad remarkably good service. A total of three orders accounted for 21 heavy Pacifics: 10 K-5s, 10 K-5as, and a lone K-5b—built in 1926, the last of the Erie's 4-6-2s. Unlike other eastern lines (notably New York Central and Lackawanna), Erie didn't advance to Hudson or 4-8-4 Northern types for passenger service; it was content with its big Pacifics until it replaced them with diesels after World War II.

OPPOSITE PAGE: In the 1940s, the Erie Railroad was a handsome property; notice the neatly trimmed ballast and well-groomed right of way. The eastward *Erie Limited* passes Lanesboro, Pennsylvania, as it works the grade to Gulf Summit on April 20, 1941. *Donald W. Furler*

Boston & Albany J-2b Hudson 606 was westbound at Palmer, Massachusetts, on Independence Day 1945. This was one of 20 Hudson types built for New York Central's New England affiliate. *Robert A. Buck*

New York Central's stream-lined J-3a Hudsons were among the finest locomotives to ever work American rails. This one leads the Empire State Express. *John E. Pickett*

Hudsons

New York Central connected several of America's most populous cities, and it was the penultimate passenger carrier, second only to its archrival, Pennsylvania Railroad. Despite the advent of the automobile, the railroad continued to enjoy passenger growth through the 1920s. By mid-decade, Central's modern Pacifics were straining to maintain schedules with its heaviest trains. To cope with traffic growth, the railroad often ran its named passenger trains in multiple sections (this was a steam-era practice where more than one train was used to cover a schedule move, each train set being known as a "section" of the named train). Thus on busy days, Central's famed flagship, the *20th Century Limited* (a first-class, extra-fare, New York–Chicago nonstop train), might require two or more sections, and these would follow one another over the length of the railroad. But double heading and operating multiple sections was an expensive way to accommodate traffic surges, since one of the most expensive parts of operating trains was labor, and in the 1920s labor costs were rising rapidly.

The 4-6-2 offered a nearly ideal type of locomotive. It was fast, powerful, and smooth running, perfect for the early years of steel passenger cars. By the 1920s, New York Central

Boston & Albany's Hudson 613 is seen at rapid pace leading train 78 east of Warren, Massachusetts, on June 7, 1949.
Robert A. Buck

New York Central's westward *Empire State Express* sprints along the Mohawk Division at milepost 194 in 1948. Leading the long consist is a high-stepping J1 Hudson. *John E. Pickett*

advertised its passenger service as its "Great Steel Fleet." Nevertheless, the railroad still needed longer trains that could operate at sustained high speeds, having pushed the Pacific design to its effective limits.

New York Central was an unusual case; many of its key mainlines were engineered very early and as a result faced abnormally restrictive clearances that limited the size of its motive power. While clearance restrictions were less of problem in the nineteenth century, they limited the design of big-boiler

Pacific types. Central's top passenger locomotives needed to be agile and strong; they were able to get up to speed, typically 75–80 mph, and stay there for mile after mile with a heavy train in tow. That was a lot to ask of a locomotive, especially when the line hemmed in.

The key to this puzzle was the introduction of a four-wheel radial trailing truck, an innovation that made it possible to design an extra-large, high-capacity boiler capable of supplying enormous volumes of steam at sustained high speeds (see

Chapter 3). While Lima first applied the four-wheel radial to high-horsepower freight locomotives in the mid-1920s, Alco worked closely with New York Central to develop new passenger types, the first of which was the 4-6-4. In 1926, Paul Kiefer was New York Central's top locomotive designer. He had an exceptional understanding of modern locomotive practices and drafted plans for a 4-6-4 locomotive that expanded on the railroad's most modern 4-6-2. Fittingly, the wheel arrangement was named for the Hudson River, whose shoreline New York Central hugged for 125 miles on its famed water-level run between New York City and Albany.

Keifer gradually honed the 4-6-4 into the ultimate six-coupled locomotive. New York Central continued to improve on it for the next dozen years and operated the best and largest fleet of this thoroughbred type.

The locomotive's wheel arrangement provided the foundation for key improvements: a larger firebox with a bigger boiler and perfectly balanced high-speed running gear. Central's first class of Hudson, J-1a, offered ample firebox capacity that was roughly 20 percent greater than its most modern Pacific.

Kiefer knew that as a premier passenger engine, the Hudson needed both high performance and a handsome appearance to lead its finest trains. In response, Kiefer drafted a well-proportioned and balanced locomotive. The March 1927 issue of *Railway and Locomotive Engineering* used the term "stream line" to describe the engine's appearance (although in the mid-1920s this had not yet come to infer art deco styling and aerodynamic designs). Unlike some other modern locomotives, which were characterized by immodest appearances and featured unsightly appendages hanging from their boilers or mounted awkwardly on their smokeboxes, the Hudson's auxiliary plumbing was largely concealed beneath locomotive boiler jacketing. (In the mid-1930s, New York Central's Hudsons would be the first steam locomotives to be dressed in sleek streamlined shrouds; later Hudsons would receive a variety of shrouded treatments.) The very first 4-6-4 New York Central class J-1a, 5200, was delivered on Valentine's Day in 1927.

Alfred Bruce, author of *The Steam Locomotive in America*, states that "when exhaustive comparative road tests were made, it was found that the 4-6-4-type produced 24 percent more drawbar horsepower and a 26 percent higher speed than did the 4-6-2 type—and that was the whole answer."

A tide of Hudsons followed. Over the next four years, New York Central received 205 J-1 Hudsons, all built by Alco between 1927 and 1931. There were some notable refinements: where the early locomotives used Walschaerts valve gear, the later ones instead had Baker gear, which allowed for superior control of engine output. Central's Boston & Albany received a variation, classed J-2, with slightly smaller drivers that better suited B&A's Berkshire grades. The most refined Hudson came ten years after the first. In his book *A Practical Evaluation of Railroad Motive Power*, Kiefer explained, "It has been our endeavor for succeeding reciprocating steam designs steadily to decrease weight per horsepower developed and to increase the steam generating plant and drawbar pull capacities and overall thermal efficiencies"—in other words, to get more power with less locomotive and achieve greater efficiency. The resulting class J-3a delivered 875 more horsepower than the J-1 and could deliver its peak output, 4,725 horsepower, at 75 mph.

Several New York Central Hudsons were treated with streamlined shrouds. The most famous was made in 1938, when industrial designer Henry Dreyfuss styled J-3a Hudsons with classic art deco sheathing, a treatment designed to coincide with the debut of the all-new streamlined *20th Century Limited*.

RIGHT: Nickel Plate's 4-6-4s began as passenger engines, but in their final years they were assigned to "universal service" and often worked way freights. Engine No. 174 leading short freight waits on a siding in eastern Ohio in the early 1950s.
J. William Vigrass

Nickel Plate Road's 175 has attracted a few admirers in this early 1950s view in Cleveland, Ohio. The application of smoke deflectors gave Nickel Plate's Hudsons a distinctive appearance.
J. William Vigrass

HUDSON DIVERSITY

Soon after New York Central, more railroads placed orders for 4-6-4s. The type was ultimately operated by lines all across the continent from Canada to Mexico and from Maine to southern California. The Hudson type, however, was never as widely built as the Pacific type; in total, just 19 railroads operated Hudsons and fewer than 500 4-6-4s were built in North America compared to an estimated 6,000 4-6-2s.

Nickel Plate Road ran relatively few long-distance trains, yet was quick to adopt the 4-6-4, receiving four from Alco just a few months after New York Central's pioneer engine. Lima built four more in 1929. On most railroads, Hudsons were strictly passenger locomotives, but while Nickel Plate's 4-6-4 began as passenger engines, in their later years they were assigned to "universal service" and often worked freight trains.

Some railroads only sampled the type. Delaware, Lackawanna & Western bought a small fleet of 4-6-4s in 1938; Canadian National ordered five; and Maine Central took two from Baldwin. Illinois Central created the most peculiar of all 4-6-4s, a home-built machine that was converted from a 2-8-4 specifically for freight service, making it the only Hudson not intended for passenger service.

HIAWATHA STREAMLINED HUDSON

In the late 1930s, Milwaukee Road ran some really fast trains; some authorities have hinted that its *Hiawatha* routinely hit as high as 120 mph to maintain tight schedules on the Chicago–Twin Cities run. This was not a one-time show aimed only at impressing visitors on a press run, but business as usual. Imagine the sight of a sleek, streamlined Hudson racing across Wisconsin dairyland at such speeds!

Milwaukee's magnificent *Hiawatha* remains one of the highpoints of twentieth-century steam power. The concept for the railroad's superfast steam-powered streamliner was a reaction to the recent debut of rapid internal combustion–powered lightweight passenger trains. Burlington's *Zephyr* had dazzled the public and awed travelers and railroad executives alike. Soon after widely publicized test runs, Burlington prepared for a pair of *Zephyrs* to work Chicago–Twin Cities services. This was a competitive market, so Milwaukee looked to match the performance of these new trains by using a lightweight train of its own design (powered by highly refined, conventional, Alco-built steam locomotives) rather than dabbling with diesels.

Milwaukee Road's streamlined *Hiawatha* was perhaps the fastest train ever scheduled to be hauled by steam. The first of its Alco-built Hudsons was brand new when photographed at Chicago on October 14, 1938. *John E. Pickett collection*

Milwaukee had been following trends in modern locomotive development; it was among the early railroads to adopt modern 4-6-4s. These were its F6 class, built by Baldwin in 1930. On July 20, 1934, Milwaukee demonstrated the capabilities of steam-powered, high-speed passenger service by assigning F6 4-6-4 to 6402 to a special train that raced from Chicago to Milwaukee in just 67 minutes, 35 seconds, maintaining a very high average speed of 90 mph over 68.9 miles.

Despite using a 4-6-4 in tests, for its initial new *Hiawatha* service locomotives, Milwaukee reverted to the older 4-4-2 Atlantic wheel arrangement. Alco built four supremely streamlined A-class 4-4-2s, which proved to be outstanding machines. They were capable of working exceptionally fast schedules where they routinely hit speeds of more than 110 mph.

The *Hiawatha*'s immediate success outpaced the ability for the 4-4-2s to maintain schedules with longer consists, so Milwaukee returned to Alco for a big, fast, streamlined engine. Alco delivered six elegant, streamlined Hudsons to Milwaukee Road in August 1938, designated as its F7 class; they had a streamlining treatment that was similar to that of the A-class Atlantics. In November 1938, *Railway Mechanical Engineer* profiled the locomotive, crediting its styling as a joint effort of Milwaukee's engineers, Alco, and industrial designer Otto Kuhler, who styled many of Alco's streamlined locomotives.

Milwaukee's F7s were exceptionally well-built locomotives with many noteworthy attributes, making them the very embodiment of modern steam design. The F7's 7-foot diameter, cast-steel Boxpok driving wheels were some of the tallest applied to any American locomotive. Notably, the engines used a General Steel Castings Corp. cast-steel bed that featured vital equipment, including integral cylinders. Alloyed-steel reciprocating parts and multiple bearing crossheads were designed for working at sustained high speeds.

Where the Atlantics were built for the Chicago–Twin Cities *Hiawatha* run, the six F7 Hudsons operated in wider territory and handled a variety of long-distance trains, including transcontinental services such as the *Olympian*, which brought them as far west as Harlowton, Montana.

LONG-DISTANCE SPRINTERS

Atchison, Topeka & Santa Fe embraced late-era steam locomotive design; some of these engines were among the most refined and impressive to operate in the United States. These were characterized by large-boiler, high-output designs, with four-wheel trailing trucks and modern equipment, including lightweight alloy-steel reciprocating equipment and other innovations. Three types of late-era Santa Fe locomotives warrant special consideration: its 4-6-4 Hudsons, 4-8-4 Northerns, and 2-10-4 Texas types (the latter two types are covered in Chapters 3 and 4, respectively).

Santa Fe's locomotive classification was peculiar compared to many American railroads. While most roads grouped similar locomotives using an alphabetic or alphanumeric system, Santa Fe assigned engines of a specific design to a common numbering series and referred to them by a numeric class starting with the first locomotive in the sequence. Generally speaking, it grouped locomotives with similar wheel arrangements and operating characteristics sequentially. Santa Fe's early classes of Pacifics were numbered in the 1200 and 1300 series, and its later Pacifics were largely placed in the 3400 and 3500 series. Although Santa Fe's system followed a logical arrangement, it could cause some confusion, especially when the number of the first locomotive of a particular class didn't begin at an expected place. Its first class of Hudsons, for example, followed a group of Pacifics and thus began in the 3450 series.

Santa Fe's investment in the latest modern steam design took a leap forward with 10 4-6-4 Hudsons built in 1927. Ten years later, it received six thoroughbred Hudsons in its 3460-number series that provided some of its most impressive service. These were conceived for service on its premier transcontinental passenger trains. Interestingly, Santa Fe had already sampled its first passenger diesels, and so these supermodern Hudsons had to rival diesel performance. Their 7-foot-tall driving wheels, which towered above anyone on a railway platform, were made for sustained fast running across the plains and deserts of the West.

The 3460s performed well on exceptionally long runs. During World War I, Santa Fe had begun to push the limits of locomotive endurance by lengthening the runs of locomotives operating through several consecutive districts. The success of this practice resulted in the railroad gradually increasing the maximum run of some locomotives. By the late 1930s, Santa Fe locomotives had some of the longest regular runs in the United States.

On December 9, 1937, Santa Fe staged a special publicity trip from Los Angeles to Chicago with Hudson 3461 that set the world's record for the longest continuous steam run.

In their prime, Santa Fe's 3460 class Hudsons clocked more than 15,000 miles a month. Engine 3463, pictured here on April 4, 1949, at Chillicothe, Illinois, was preserved and may run again. *John E. Pickett collection*

But this was the exception to the rule—more typical for its Hudsons was the run from Dearborn Station in Chicago to La Junta, Colorado.

In his book, *Railroads at War*, S. Kip Farrington wrote that in July 1942, Santa Fe's passenger locomotives were rolling an average of 318 miles per day, with some locomotives clocking 20,000 miles per month. This was an extraordinary performance that demanded intensive maintenance to ensure high reliability since running engines to the point where they would break down would have been counterproductive.

CANADIAN PACIFIC'S ROYAL HUDSONS

A name can make a locomotive famous. Perhaps the most famous of all Canadian steam locomotives were Canadian Pacific Railway's Royal Hudsons. These have become so well known they have virtually eclipsed most other modern CP steam. Yet the Royal Hudsons weren't the first or only Hudsons on the railroad. Canadian Pacific Railroad adopted the type in 1929, and, after New York Central, it operated the second-largest fleet in North America, a total of 65 locomotives.

British-born Henry Blain Bowen (1884–1965) designed 4-6-4s for CPR with large-diameter driving wheels and excellent riding qualities. This final 4-6-4 development captured public attention. Alco's Canadian subsidiary, Montreal Locomotive Works, built a fleet of semi-streamlined engines between 1937 and 1940. However, it wasn't until after two of the class, engines 2850 and 2852, hauled Britain's King George VI and Queen Elizabeth across Canada in 1939 that these 4-6-4s were named Royal Hudsons. To signify the importance of their royal duties, the whole fleet of late-build streamlined Hudsons were so designated and decorated with an embossed crown.

LEFT: What could be more majestic than a Royal Hudson at speed? On November 10, 1956, Canadian Pacific 2823 was hitting 90 mph on its run from Montreal to Quebec City. *Jim Shaughnessy*

OPPOSITE: A restored Canadian Pacific Royal Hudson works at Horseshoe Bay, British Columbia, on October 4, 1975. *George W. Kowanski*

Eight-Coupled Engines: The Backbone of Twentieth-Century Railroads

IN THE TWENTIETH CENTURY, the eight-coupled engine assumed the role held by the four-coupled engine in the nineteenth century. As with most changes to railroading, this was a gradual but irreversible evolution.

While the 4-4-0 dominated transportation in the latter half of the nineteenth century, various eight-coupled types began to assume the dominant position in the twentieth as big locomotives became the new standard power.

Eight-coupled power wasn't a twentieth-century phenomenon, but in the new century a handful of new types represented by dozens of classes (and tens of thousands of individual locomotives) rolled forth as the backbone of American railroad transportation. Six-coupled types, predominantly 4-6-0, 4-6-2s, and 4-6-4s, dominated passenger work, while the eight-coupled types moved freight. There were, of course, many exceptions, some of which are highlighted in these pages; nevertheless, the eight-coupled freight locomotive was the real money earner. In the twentieth century, freight business represented the majority of traffic on many lines and was certainly the largest revenue generator in the industry as a whole. So

while the high-profile six-coupled types may have been more familiar to the general public due to their high-profile assignments on passenger trains, it was the legions of eight-coupled machines that really paid the bills.

In the final decades of steam production, eight-coupled types in the form of 4-8-2s and 4-8-4s were developed both for general service (freight and passenger work) and for some exceptionally capable passenger service. Toward the end of the steam era, many of the largest railroads focused on highly refined eight-coupled steam for heavy passenger work, and the

4-8-4 type was on its way to becoming a universal mainline locomotive before it was dethroned by the diesel-electric.

The 2-8-4 Berkshire type, only represented by some 750 engines, has a special place in late-era steam. It was the first example of Lima's Superpower concept, which was a pivotal development in the final decades of steam production.

The combined fleets of eight-coupled types greatly outnumbered all other types, with the 2-8-0 and 2-8-2 being by far the most numerous. The 2-8-0's origins were in the nineteenth century; while it was a big machine for its day and

Milwaukee Road class S-2 4-8-4 201 works west through suburban Chicago at Elgin, Illinois, on July 5, 1953. *John E. Pickett*

built in vast numbers (more than 33,000 were constructed for domestic service and export), most were relatively small in comparison with the larger eight-coupled types developed in the twentieth century. A few railroads remained loyal to the 2-8-0, however, and some of the later engines had relatively large dimensions.

Locomotives at Work

For the ordinary person living in the steam era, engines were often viewed as a part of life's daily backdrop. You may have caught a glimpse of a column of exhaust rising in the distance across a cornfield, seen a cloud of smoke moving from beyond a row of trees or over the tops of houses, or heard a distant whistle as an engine approached a road crossing. At the station, an engine whirled past in a hiss of steam, smelling of soot, cinders, and grease. You may have taken such a train to work, to go on vacation, visit relatives, seek your fortune, or as you went off to war.

Freight trains were also part of the landscape in any industrialized town or city. Switch engines could be heard slamming

BELOW: When steam ruled the rails, hardly anyone gave scenes like this a second glance. An Ohio Central photographers' charter is put on film at Morgan Run, Ohio, on October 18, 2003. *Chris Bost*

Dramatic lighting makes for a timeless portrait of former Grand Trunk Western 6325 on an Ohio Central photographers' charter on October 18, 2003. *Chris Bost*

cars in the yards, their whistles sounding short blasts as they moved back and forth. Big engines could be seen hammering across viaducts, through fields, or even down the streets of towns where the tracks shared the public road.

And yet, for the most part, ordinary people were no more impressed by the sight and sound of steam engines than people today are by the sight of a delivery truck or a jet passing overhead. Whether a locomotive had 4 wheels or 20 was of little concern. Whether it was a common type or a modern thoroughbred didn't matter. The locomotives were here, there, and everywhere; they were an ordinary part of every day, and they blended into the background of life.

But for railroaders, locomotives were the tools of their trade. Engine crews spent every working day in and around steam locomotives, more often than not working on the footplate—the precarious position in the cab from where the locomotive was fed and run. The engineer, with eyes forward, hand on the throttle, controlled the power and force of the machine. He held the responsibility for making the engine move, and more important, ensuring it stopped again safely. The fireman fed the insatiable machine by shoveling coal into its belly or manipulating equipment (often in the form a stoker) to deliver fuel mechanically. He ensured its boiler was at the right level and kept a sharp eye on the sight glass to make sure the water never got too low; if it did, the result could be catastrophic—a boiler explosion was a greatly feared event.

BELOW: Grand Trunk Western class U3b 4-8-4 number 6325 works an Ohio Central photographers' charter near Pearl, Ohio, on October 18, 2003. *Chris Bost*

Trailing view of GTW 6325 near Pearl, Ohio, on October 18, 2003. *Chris Bost*

At the sprawling repair shops and locomotive factories, legions of workers built and tended to the engines. They crafted metal into machines and brought engines to life. They forged, cast, fabricated, and assembled iron and steel into highly refined contraptions that were the engines of a nation. Steam locomotives required daily maintenance. From the time they emerged from the shop as new machines to the day they were drained and left cold, locomotives required almost constant attention. Every day before an engine left the roundhouse, its fire would be tended, the boiler brought up to pressure, tender filled with fuel and water, and sanders on the engine filled.

At the end of the run, or as needed en route, ashes were dumped, boilers flushed, and machinery inspected and, if necessary, repaired. An operating crew might have reported a leaking injector, a bearing that seemed to be running hot, or any number of small faults in the running gear that might need immediate attention. At regular intervals, a locomotive required heavy repair. It would be brought into the shop and taken apart and then rebuilt again in-kind (as it was).

The gods of steam were the mere mortals who, on paper, transformed metal into machines and drafted the plans for engines that converted reciprocating motion into rotary motion. They saw the future and crafted it by directing men, machines, and metal. They included Alco's Francis J. Cole, Lima's William E. Woodard, New York Central's Paul W. Kiefer, and Union Pacific's Otto Jabelmann, who not only solved the complex problems of how to make a modern locomotive, but who also pushed steam engine designs to new limits with the aim of extracting greater power and better efficiency from the external-combustion reciprocating engine, and did so within the constraints of the railroad's limited infrastructure.

MIKADO—TWENTIETH-CENTURY AMERICAN WORKHORSE

The 2-8-2 was among the first big new types that emerged in the twentieth century. By no means did it represent the very

largest engines, but it was the second-most common road locomotive after the 2-8-0. For decades, the type was ubiquitous and assigned to road freights all across the continent.

Examples of the 2-8-2 dated back to the 1860s, but the modern 2-8-2 with a large firebox and radial trailing truck was among the new large types refined after 1900. *Mikado* is an archaic word for the Japanese emperor, and the name was attached to the type when Baldwin exported some narrow-gauge 2-8-2s to Japan in 1897. At the time Gilbert & Sullivan's comic opera *Mikado* had peaked in public awareness, so while Baldwin's exports weren't the first known application of the

Central Railroad of New Jersey 2-8-2 894 leads an 82-car westward freight at Bowmanstown, Pennsylvania. The 2-8-2 Mikado was the most widely built freight steam locomotive in the twentieth century.
Donald W. Furler

2-8-2 arrangement, the honorary name seemed appropriate for this new large type.

In the United States, the name Mikado was often shortened to just Mike. And during World War II, anti-Japanese sentiment encouraged some railroads to unsuccessfully rename the 2-8-2 as the MacArthur type, in honor of the popular American general.

The first modern Mikados built for operation in the United States were comparatively compact Baldwins built in 1903 for North Dakota's Bismarck, Washburn & Great Falls Railway. Northern Pacific, which needed a powerful freight hauler, must have noticed its small neighbor's big new engines, so in 1905 NP placed a large order with Alco's Brooks Works for some hefty 2-8-2s. In the spirit of the times, these new engines fulfilled NP's desire for power, and during the next two years NP acquired 160 2-8-2s for freight service, the first large fleet. Some of these worked for nearly half a century, although they were later upgraded and equipped with superheaters and other appliances for improved efficiency.

The 2-8-2 wheel arrangement offered a natural progression from the 2-8-0—the type that had dominated heavy road freight work in the late nineteenth and early twentieth centuries. Great operational flexibility afforded by the 2-8-2's comparatively low axle loadings, combined with ample steam power and high tractive effort, made the Mikado the dominant type of new freight locomotive from 1910 to about 1930, during which time it gradually replaced the 2-8-0 as the standard freight hauler.

By the 1920s, if you stood trackside you were more likely to find a Mikado hauling a freight than any other type of new locomotive. However, while considered relatively big by the standards of an observer in 1910, the common Mike was soon dwarfed by a host of larger designs. In the 1920s, the large

In 1973, Southern 4501 traveled to Baraboo, Wisconsin, to pull the historic circus train based there. It is seen crossing Lake Wisconsin at Merrimac. *John Gruber*

Mikado was the basis for the development of the first Lima Superpower, the famed 2-8-4 Berkshire profiled below.

During World War I, the United States Railroad Administration drafted two plans for Mikados: "light" and "heavy" varieties that differed in weight by about 14 tons and together represented the vast majority of USRA types built for American lines. (See discussion of the USRA on page 75.)

Pennsylvania Railroad adopted the 2-8-2 in 1914 and over the next five years acquired some 574 virtually identical Class L1s Mikados (small s for "superheated"). As mentioned in Chapter 2, these shared many common components with

OPPOSITE: Illinois Central was among the last railroads to operate big steam in revenue service. Mountain-type 2524 leads a coal train upgrade at Paducah, Kentucky, in February 1960. *Ron Wright*

PRR's K4s Pacific type. Some were built by the railroad's Juniata Shops in Altoona; others were supplied by Lima or Baldwin. While PRR's large fleet of L1s 2-8-2 locomotives was impressive, New York Central System had the greatest fleet of Mikados, nearly 1,400 of the type grouped into a host of sub-classes. While PRR was satisfied with a single uniform design and took pride in its fleet of standard types, Central was continually refining its locomotive, aiming to improve performance and efficiency with every order for new equipment.

Yet as common as they were on some lines, several notable railroads never bought Mikes. Boston & Maine, Delaware & Hudson, and Norfolk & Western could be seen as Mikado-free zones. D&H was among proponents of the 2-8-0 Consolidation, and under the administration of Leonor F. Loree, it continued to refine this older wheel arrangement into the 1920s. Its peculiar high-pressure compounds were intended to achieve new levels of thermal efficiency using reciprocating steam locomotives. Four were built, but they proved short lived. For its final steam acquisitions, D&H bought modern Challengers and 4-8-4s, yet many of its older 2-8-0s worked right to the end of its steam operations in 1953.

However, for photographers seeking big American steam, catching a lone Mikado wasn't much of a prize. Not when there were large articulateds, 2-10-2s, and ever-larger eight-coupled types on the move.

Traffic, Infrastructure, and Motive Power in the Boom Years

Looking back at the American steam locomotive, many observers have tended to focus on the engines in their final years, the period from the beginning of the Great Depression through the Cold War–era, when the railroad companies were facing a difficult transition, complicated by the specter of being overwhelmed by highway competition.

Often forgotten is the situation that faced American railroads during the first three decades of the twentieth century, including the conditions that precipitated crucial changes to railroad technology and how they affected motive power development and railroad operations. These were years characterized by unparalleled growth and complicated by larger economic changes that resulted in spiraling costs and the rise of new competition, all conditions that precipitated the difficulties experienced in later years.

America grew rapidly after the Civil War, and by the turn of the twentieth century, railroads were facing continued tides of traffic that saturated their lines, limiting their ability to keep pace with traffic growth. Complicating matters were the different operating characteristics of freight and passenger traffic, an issue exacerbated by dramatic increases of traffic to both, combined with demands for ever faster and safer trains. As the century matured, these problems would come to a head.

Since the late nineteenth century, heavy and slow-moving "drag" freights had been the rule on many American mainlines. Railroads had resisted moving freight faster because moving heavy trains at greater speed required substantially more fuel. There were also safety concerns. Getting tonnage up to speed was one thing; stopping it again was another problem altogether. As a result, despite the gradual increase in locomotive power, most advances to freight power focused on larger engines and involved moving more tonnage at the same slow speeds.

The massive Mallet compounds (see Chapter 5) and other big haulers were not fast engines and rarely needed to operate faster than about 20 mph in revenue service. By 1910, while the average length of trains was much greater than a half-century earlier, the speed of freights hadn't improved significantly and rarely exceeded an average of 8–12 mph.

After a while, the old philosophy of simply adding more cars to freight trains reached the point of diminishing returns. As traffic swelled, increasing numbers of drag freights caused mainlines to congeal. Longer freights required more power, which was especially problematic in steeply graded territory where helper locomotives were needed to assist heavy trains. Not only were helper operations costly, but taking helpers on and off and running helper engines back to the bottom of the grade further impeded track capacity.

As trains grew longer, they threatened to exceed the limits of existing infrastructure, specifically the length of yard tracks and passing sidings. There were ways around these impediments. Long freights could "double out of the yard," meaning the locomotive would pull forward with the first half of the train, then reverse back into the yard to collect the second portion. Only once it was all together could the freight proceed. This was time consuming and further strained yard capacity.

Slow freights were forever getting in the way of passenger trains and limiting the capacity of mainlines. This situation was compounded as railroads began to run faster passenger trains. Railroads needed to improve fluidity; in other words, they had to make mainlines function better to handle greater volumes of traffic. One solution was to build more track—installing bigger yards, lengthening passing sidings, or adding more mainline tracks.

In the early twentieth century, railroad companies had had greater access to capital, and the largest railroads addressed traffic problems by making massive investments in infrastructure to expand capacity. Lines were straightened, mountain grades were relocated to ease operations, bridges and tracks were upgraded to allow for heavier locomotives and rolling stock, and new larger yards were built to enable the building and breakdown of larger freights. Systems with the heaviest

traffic, such as the Baltimore & Ohio, New Haven, New York Central, and Pennsylvania Railroads, had invested in multiple-track mainlines, which not only increased capacity by providing more track space but enabled the separation of slow-moving trains, such as drag freights, from faster traffic. While this proved to be one of the most effective means of solving traffic problems, it was also one of the most costly.

Two significant advances had occurred to vastly improve the safe movement of trains and allow for operation of faster trains while increasing line capacity. This was the industry-wide implementation of automatic air brakes and the limited introduction of automatic block signaling systems. Interestingly, the railroads had fiercely resisted the universal implementation of automatic air brakes because of the enormous cost of equipping trains, yet this proved to be one of the most important innovations in regard to industry operations.

Automatic air brakes allowed the locomotive engineer to set brakes throughout the train, and this offered a quantum leap in train handling. Before automatic braking, trains relied entirely on brakemen riding on the cars to set and release the brakes on a signal from the engineer. Not only was this practice extraordinarily dangerous for the individual brakeman, but it severely limited the speed and length of freight trains.

By 1917, railroad companies felt the combined pinch of rapidly rising wages and record volumes of heavy traffic (both caused in part by World War I). They were also facing rapidly growing highway competition, which had begun to siphon away some of the most lucrative traffic. Together, these changes resulted in the collapse of the network's ability to function normally.

Although it may not have been obvious at the time, the railroad's problems were magnified due to unanticipated consequences of early twentieth-century antitrust legislation. By

1914, the fallout from these laws effectively put major capital investments out of reach.

Short-term efforts to solve traffic problems proved ineffective. Then, in April 1917, America's direct involvement in World War I rapidly compounded railroad traffic problems. The entire nation was spurred into action, but the railroad network was already beyond its capacity to handle traffic effectively, and soon it suffered from complete gridlock.

By the end of year, President Wilson deemed it necessary for the government to assume operation of the railroads and sort out the traffic quagmire as a wartime emergency. The United States Railroad Administration was formed to do the job. In the 1920s, operation of the railroads was returned to their private owners. Most of the details of USRA operations are beyond the scope of this book, but one significant action it undertook was an effort to standardize locomotive design. The USRA oversaw development of a dozen standard types, some of which continued to positively influence steam locomotive production and development after American railroads returned to private ownership.

Following the traumatic years of USRA control and a calming of the traffic situation, America's railroads resumed their efforts to improve operations while benefiting from the postwar prosperity of the 1920s. But the war had accelerated development of the automotive industry, and railroads faced a continued erosion of high-value, time-sensitive traffic. In response, they renewed their efforts toward lowering costs, raising freight speeds, and easing traffic congestion.

It was the last summer for steam on the Pennsylvania Railroad; on August 6, 1957 the railroad's impressive class M1 Mountain is seen on the turntable at Elmira, New York. *Ron Wright*

Southern Railway 2-8-2 4501 climbs Duncan Hill toward a tunnel in Indiana in 1966, pulling excursion trains out of Louisville during the first days of its return to service. *John Gruber*

David P. Morgan and Steam

by JOHN GRUBER

David P. Morgan not only told the story of the economic necessity for diesel locomotives in his editorial columns in *Trains* magazine, but he and his wife, Margaret, frequently traveled to ride behind steam locomotives, especially in his native South.

His interest in steam showed up early, when he wrote about Santa Fe "Glamour Girl 3461." "What has this pin-up of mine done, you ask? 3461 works in no studio, but can be seen racing across Illinois and Kansas at eighty miles an hour—that's her stage," he said during World War II in November 1944 in his high school literary magazine in Louisville. (The Coalition for Sustainable Rail plans to use a similar locomotive, no. 3463, to test modern technology and biofuels.)

As editor of *Trains* from 1953 to 1987, Morgan chronicled the transition from steam to diesel. The 33 articles he wrote from April 1954 to November 1958—a series with titles such as "Steam in Indian Summer"—came together in a book entitled *The Mohawk that Refused to Abdicate and Other Tales* (1975). A quiet person, he appears by his account anonymously in 16 photos in the volume, often in unassuming poses in the shadows.

More telling, on the 25th anniversary of their travels together, he declined a proposal from photographer Phil Hastings for a new search "for Little Joe electrics, aging F and FA cab units, due-to-be-phased-out FMs." Writing in his epilogue, he noted, "I don't dislike diesels (or electrics); but I do have them departmentalized in my mind. To have sought to chronicle them in the same manner as we did 3005, 4008, 136, 5403, 4501, 754, and company would somehow have contaminated the memory and the recording of our other searches."

He had already turned his attention to Southern Railway 4501, which he had visited on a short line at Stearns, Kentucky. No. 4501 was built by Baldwin Locomotive Works in Philadelphia in 1911. Morgan was with the locomotive when it returned to Chattanooga in 1964 for rebuilding and in 1966 when it made its shakedown trip from Chattanooga to Louisville and back to Asheville, Spencer, and Richmond. I was along as the photographer.

Of course he returned to many other locomotives, such as Louisville & Nashville 152, a 1905 Pacific preserved at the Kentucky Railroad Museum. After riding behind it, he said in "Weep no more, my lady" (*Trains*, November 1986), "I had never, never expected the Old Reliable to return in steam, much less in this guise or this gusto." Morgan had been fond of the L&N since his high school days in Louisville. He also wrote about the return to service of Southern and Norfolk Southern locomotives through streamlined NS 611 in 1982, headlining his article ". . . and the last first" (a reference to Mark 10:31) and saying that the last Norfolk & Western J is first among steam locomotives today.

But the best is reserved for *Locomotive 4501* (1968), a book based on the 1966 journey. He concludes with words that would be repeated many times over: "Margaret, pack the bags. We're going south to meet an old friend of the family. You remember—the lady from Philadelphia."

Southern 4501 stands next to the train sheds at Terminal Station in Chattanooga in 1966, ready to depart on its first trip after restoration. *John Gruber*

New York Central operated the largest fleet of 4-8-2s but called them Mohawks rather than Mountains. Central's L-2d 2967 works an empty train of refrigerated box-cars on Central's four-track Mohawk Division.
Robert W. Witbeck

MOUNTAINS

Mountains. Just the name invokes an image of a big engine; yet the Mountain type was more about speed than size. In 1910, Chesapeake & Ohio pushed nonarticulated design, and the resulting 4-8-2 type seemed large. This engine had one more driving axle than a Pacific and rode high on the rails. C&O developed the 4-8-2 to avoid the cost of double heading heavy passenger trains over the Allegheny Mountains and in effect melded the best qualities of the low-driver 2-8-2 Mikado and high-driver 4-6-2 Pacific for passenger service.

The first 4-8-2s were delivered in 1911. The October 1911 *Railway & Locomotive Engineering* profiled the new locomotive, describing it as "a new type of passenger locomotive, the most powerful in the world." And in detailing its performance on C&O's graded territory, the journal said, "Mr. J. E. Walsh, superintendent of motive power [at C&O], has appropriately

ABOVE: Old Boston & Maine 4-8-2 4101 is a long way from home. In 1947, B&M sold this engine to Baltimore & Ohio, where it became 5651, seen here on B&O rails with a Q-4 Mikado hauling freight at Attica Junction, Ohio. *George C. Corey*

New York Central's Mohawks were built for fast freight; on a frigid winter's day, L-2c 2739 makes a volcanic display as it accelerates eastward on the Mohawk Division. *Robert W. Witbeck*

named them the 'mountain type.'" It continued, "[the 4-8-2s] have not only surpassed the expectations of the builders in the point of power and speed, but they have exceeded the expectation of the [C&O] in point of economy, so that the continuation of this new type is already a forgone certainty."

Alco placed advertisements boasting of C&O's 4-8-2s capabilities: "the new locomotive hauls trains of ten and twelve cars over the Virginia mountains at higher speed than an ordinary locomotive can make with six cars."

However, unlike the Pacific type, which had gained rapid acceptance a decade earlier, the new Mountain was relatively slow to catch on. But its advantages were gradually recognized, and ultimately an estimated 2,400 were built, with production of the 4-8-2 continuing until after World War II, longer than most other pre–World War II types.

The 4-8-2 was designed for high-horsepower applications, meaning it was designed to deliver its maximum output at higher speeds. So while a 2-10-2 or Mallet was designed for heavy freight service with maximum power produced at 8–12 mph, a Mountain was intended to work upgrade at 25 mph and clip along on level track at 50 mph or more. The Mountain was originally developed for passenger service, but soon some railroads engineered the type as a fast freight locomotive.

New York Central proved especially fond of the 4-8-2—although it called them Mohawks—and refined the type to an exceptionally powerful freight hauler. It adopted the type relatively early and continued to refine it years after more advanced types (notably the 4-8-4, discussed below) dominated purchases of fast eight-coupled engines on other railroads. Ultimately, it refined the type into a dual-traffic engine, and its later Mohawks worked both fast freight and its Great Steel Fleet. New York Central eventually bought more than any other American railroad.

In 1923, Pennsylvania Railroad introduced a new Mountain type, class M1. This was an advancement of its already successful I1s 2-10-0 Decapod (see Chapter 4). In the tradition of PRR's practice of standardization, the M1 shared many of the same components with the I1s. PRR acquired 201 M1s; some were built at the railroad's Juniata Shops in Altoona, and others were built by Baldwin and Lima. In 1930, it ordered another 100 4-8-2s that were more advanced than the original; these were designated M1a.

Three-Cylinder Mountains

In 1922, Alco introduced a modern three-cylinder locomotive concept that used a high-capacity boiler feeding two outside cylinders (connected to drive wheels in the conventional manner) and a middle cylinder driving an inside main-rod to a cranked axle. Dividing boiler output over three cylinders reduced stress on reciprocating parts and improved torque. With a three-cylinder design, the locomotive had six impulses (as a result of greater division between impulse points), so the angle between the pulses was reduced, which allowed for more uniform application of torque and a substantial increase in tractive effort without a substantial increase in engine weight.

While Alco's three-cylinder concept was applied to several locomotive designs, the greater weight as a result of the center cylinder made it well suited to the 4-8-2 type. Delaware, Lackawanna & Western, Lehigh Valley, and New Haven Railroad were among the lines that invested in these advanced 4-8-2 locomotives.

New Haven's engines were very unusual and also featured water-tube fireboxes and a one-piece cast smokebox to eliminate air leaks. *Railway Mechanical Engineer* reported that "increasing demand for expeditious handling of traffic on the New Haven has made greater speed in the movement of freight

On November 28, 1946, Delaware, Lackawanna & Western 4-8-4 1644 leads train 3, the *Lackawanna Limited* westbound under catenary at Summit, New Jersey. *Donald W. Furler*

essential." These specially designed 4-8-2s were intended for fast freight service between Boston, Massachusetts, and the large interchange yard west of the Hudson River at Maybrook, New York. On the run from Cedar Hill Yard (near New Haven, Connecticut) to Maybrook, they were expected to haul 100 loaded freight cars weighing 5,000 tons at passenger train speeds. This was a tall order for any locomotive of the period.

THE BIRTH OF SUPERPOWERED STEAM

Lima was an up-and-coming builder. While not new to the steam locomotive business, its early products were largely specialized Shay-type geared engines rather than conventional locomotives. In 1912, the company changed its direction and began construction of switchers and soon moved to building mainline locomotives. During World War I, Lima thrived and rapidly earned the position of America's third-largest steam locomotive manufacturer.

Lima's William E. Woodard was a visionary inventor who pushed the limits of American locomotive design. Before going to work for Lima in 1916, he had worked for both Alco and Baldwin, the two largest locomotive builders. As Lima's vice president of engineering, Woodard strived to not only build new steam locomotives, but to forward Lima's locomotive design. His innovations resulted in many patents.

Woodard improved both the power and efficiency of the locomotive engine, hoping that if Lima built better locomotives, it could secure a larger share of the locomotive market. Ultimately he influenced the entire industry. Instead of just increasing power by building a bigger, heavier locomotive, he increased output without dramatically increasing weight, which resulted in locomotives that could move greater tonnage at higher speeds within the confines of existing infrastructure.

His improved locomotives neatly coincided with the fundamental changes affecting the industry and its burgeoning need for faster, more efficient engines.

Advanced steam locomotive design was the most effective short-term solution for overcoming traffic problems.

New York Central and Superpower

Using its fleet of 4-8-2 Mohawks, New York Central had been a fast freight pioneer, and by moving long trains faster, it had improved operations on its Water Level Route—one of the busiest freight and passenger corridors in the United States.

By the early 1920s, Central aimed to expand fast freight service on its busy and heavily graded Boston & Albany route. This was the old Western Railroad of Massachusetts and faced a famously difficult series of grades—best known was its Washington Hill climb in the Berkshire Hills of

Boston & Albany A-1b Lima-built Berkshire works upgrade with an eastward freight at Warren, Massachusetts, on July 11, 1948. *Robert A. Buck*

western Massachusetts. As previously mentioned, this route had required some of America's first specialized locomotives. Although eight decades had passed since Winan's 0-8-0 Mud Diggers had worked the line, this route remained a formidable crossing. The combination of prolonged climbs and an unusually sinuous alignment had dogged operations for decades. While other railroads had more difficult mountains to climb, B&A's grades were the longest and toughest on the New York Central System, and a continual thorn in its side.

In the early years of the twentieth century, B&A was saturated with freight, and its old double-track line didn't have enough capacity to handle the business. By 1907, a full decade before the events of World War I led to USRA control, the state of Massachusetts was fed up with New York Central's ineffective operations on the B&A. An inquiry was held, and the state considered the radical move of buying the railroad back from New York Central. Ultimately, Central opted to invest in the B&A's infrastructure and made a host of improvements to aid the flow of traffic. This included some nominal line relocations on the most difficult portions of Washington Hill, installation of long passing sidings, and some strategic sections of third and fourth main tracks. In addition, they added a host of new motive power, including a fleet of Mallet Compounds and 2-10-2 Santa Fe types.

In the 1920s, Central further improved B&A and related operations by building a massive new yard south of Albany at Selkirk, New York, connecting it to existing routes using new highly engineered cutoffs (line segments designed to shorten the distance and/or gradients and curvature of older lines). By that time it employed hundreds of 2-8-2 Mikados as one of its preferred workhorses; it was a type that had a good record on the B&A. New York Central System was one of Lima's best customers, and Woodard encouraged the railroad to order

an experimental 2-8-2 Mikado based on Central's successful, modern, Alco-built 2-8-2. This engine featured some of his advanced locomotive designs and was only three tons heavier but significantly more powerful than the Alco. Central classed this new engine as its H-10.

The railroad found that the H-10 would work freight at 30–35 mph, roughly twice the speed of one of its conventional Mikados. Notably, it maintained sustained speeds for mile after mile, a feat that set it apart from all other freight locomotives.

Lima's H-10 had taken advantage of new high-tensile alloy steels. Reciprocating parts, including siderods and main rods, were made from heat-treated chrome vanadium steel. Stronger alloys meant that less metal was required; this dramatically lowered the weight of rods, which reduced damaging reciprocating forces. The H-10 also made use of several efficiency-saving devices, including a new type of superheater, an Elesco feedwater heater, to introduce preheated water to the boiler in place of an injector, conserving energy. Use of a dry pipe with front-end throttle gave the locomotive engineer improved ability to regulate steam flow from the boiler.

New York Central ordered 302 similar locomotives from Lima and Alco, representing an enormous order for a single type. Boston & Albany got eight Alco-built H-10a 2-8-2s for freight service.

Refining the H-10 was an important step in Woodard's evolutionary improvement of the eight-coupled design. Continuing his work with Central, he transformed the H-10 design into the first 2-8-4, a milestone locomotive that influenced most subsequent locomotive designs in the United States.

In his effort to boost boiler efficiency by 10–20 percent, a larger firebox was needed, and to support the greater weight, Woodard invented a load-bearing, two-axle, radial trailing truck. This was more than merely firebox support; directly

Nickel Plate Road 2-8-4 Berkshire 759 leads an excursion on the former Pennsylvania Railroad at Gallitzin, Pennsylvania, on September 13, 1970. *George W. Kowanski*

connected to the drawbar, it transmitted the whole pulling force of the locomotive. Since the prototype 2-8-4 also used a trailing truck booster, some locomotive historians have suggested that the original 2-8-4 was in fact an articulated locomotive.

To highlight the new locomotive's superlative potential, it was designated A-1, which back in the 1920s carried a connotation of quality (the first number and first letter together appeared to have meaning).

The A-1's biggest improvement over earlier designs was that it carried a significantly larger firebox grate with much greater boiler capacity without raising overall locomotive weight. It combined its big boiler with efficiency-saving devices similar to those described above. Ample steam supply allowed the locomotive to maintain higher speeds. The application of 60 percent limited cylinder cutoff limited steam admission during just a portion of the stroke, and thus enabled greater steam expansion, which both lowered cylinder back pressure at higher speeds and allowed for more efficient use of steam. Greater efficiency contributed to lower fuel consumption. Unlike older types that might run out of steam hauling a heavy train too quickly, the A-1 had plenty of steam and could move a heavy train faster than any equivalently sized type. Lima called its new design Superpower.

Lima delivered the prototype 2-8-4 to New York Central's recently opened Selkirk Yard. This distinctive-looking machine featured a front end with an Elesco feedwater heater prominently overhanging the smokebox above the headlight, its abnormally larger boiler met the roofline of the cab while a plethora of piping and accessories gave it a surly, businesslike appearance. There was no question that this locomotive was built to haul heavy freight.

Lima's A-1 Makes the Grade

New York Central and Lima staged an event to demonstrate the power of the A-1. A modern H-10 departed Selkirk eastbound on the B&A with a typical freight, then an hour or so later, the A-1 followed with a slightly heavier train in tow. As both trains worked upgrade on the B&A, the A-1's greater power allowed it to overtake the earlier freight in less than 50 miles after leaving the yard, and in so doing actually use less fuel than the H-10. This was a huge advance—there was no looking back.

The trade magazines were filled with articles boasting of the A-1's design. It became known as the Berkshire type in honor of the hills where it demonstrated its abilities. New York Central immediately ordered 25 2-8-4s for B&A, delivered in 1926. These were followed by 20 more 2-8-4s in 1927 and

a third order in 1930 for 10 refined types (which, owing to their improved appearance became known among operating crews as "sports models"). For the next two decades, Lima's Berkshires were standard freight power on the B&A.

Other railroads followed New York Central's lead. The parallel Boston & Maine bought 25 near copies of the A-1. Although functionally almost identical, these had a peculiar appearance owing to the use of externally mounted, inverted U-shaped Coffin feedwater heaters on the smokebox in place of the Elesco.

While the Berkshire type is most closely associated with lines east of the Mississippi, Santa Fe was among western railroads to run them. *John Pickett collection*

RIGHT: On February 12, 1947, Erie Berkshire 3384 has a strong head of steam leading a 99-car westward freight at Allendale, New Jersey. *Donald W. Furler*

OPPOSITE: Take a close look at the front of Lackawanna 2228—this is no ordinary locomotive, it's one of the Alco three-cylinder 4-8-2s. The steam admission to the center cylinder is controlled by a Gresley conjugated valve gear. *Donald W. Furler*

In addition, the bell and headlight were given an unusually low placement. Some observers thought they were ugly, but the locomotives meant business. After a stint on the B&M, some were sold to Southern Pacific and others to the Santa Fe.

Interestingly, the locomotive that earned its name working in New England's pastoral green hills spent its working career in the Midwest. Illinois Central purchased the A-1 prototype and followed up with an order for 50 copies.

While the early A-1s were considered fast mountain climbers, they were still limited to about 40 mph, fast enough for the B&A but not for other lines. An advancement on the 2-8-4 design resulted in the type built with taller drivers. The first of these were sold to the Erie Railroad, which in the 1930s was part of a group of lines controlled by the Van Sweringen brothers of Cleveland. Erie amassed the largest fleet, 105 locomotives, with some built by each of the three major builders. These were among the most handsome engines to work Erie rails.

Van Sweringen's associated lines, which included Chesapeake & Ohio, Nickel Plate Road, Pere Marquette, and Wheeling & Lake Erie, benefited from their Central Advisory Committee, which supplied its roads with excellent standardized locomotive designs featuring common qualities. Under this administration, the 2-8-4 enjoyed a favored status, and Van Sweringen's lines bought many of the type over the next two decades.

Nickel Plate Road began acquiring 2-8-4s with tall drivers in 1934, and it continued to buy Berkshires until 1949. Its final locomotive was also the last Lima-built steam engine. Nickel Plate routinely worked fast freight at 70 mph with 2-8-4s. Steam enthusiasts delighted in recalling how, in the 1950s, Nickel Plate Road's late-era Berkshires working on single track outpaced New York Central's diesels of the same vintage running on its parallel multiple-track Water Level Route mainlines. It was a symbolic victory.

A NORTHERN BY ANY OTHER NAME IS STILL A 4-8-4

Northern Pacific introduced the 4-8-4 in 1927, and conferred its name on the new wheel arrangement. While the type was widely adopted across the continent, the name was not. No other wheel arrangement carried more different names than the 4-8-4. On the Lackawanna they were Poconos, Canadian National called them Confederations, New York Central knew them as Niagaras, and oddly enough so did the National Railways of Mexico. On Chesapeake & Ohio they were Greenbriers, while Nashville, Chattanooga & St. Louis referred to their 4-8-4s as Dixies, and so on.

87

ABOVE LEFT: Robert B. Claytor speaks to a large crowd assembled in Roanoke in 1982 to welcome N&W 611. He called it "the finest steam passenger engine built, anywhere, anytime." *John Gruber*

ABOVE: Fireman's view shows the streamlined jacket of N&W 611 on its return home to Roanoke in 1982. *John Gruber*

LEFT: On the first day of its return to service, surrounded by kudzu, N&W 611 passes a Coke sign in the Deep South. *John Gruber*

ABOVE: On October 15, 1993, Cotton Belt 4-8-4 819 storms through the searchlight block signals near Gilmer, Texas, working at 60 mph toward the Tyler Rose Festival. *Tom Kline*

ABOVE RIGHT: Early morning fog turns to haze as Cotton Belt 819 gallops across the girder deck span over the tranquil Saline River west of Rison, Arkansas, on October 15, 1993. The locomotive is leading an excursion to Tyler, Texas, 282 miles distant. *Tom Kline*

RIGHT: Delaware & Hudson was one of several railroads that employed "elephant ear"–style smoke-lifters to improve the airflow around the engine. In April 1953, D&H 4-8-4 308 leads freight RW-6 at Plattsburg, New York. *Jim Shaughnessy*

TOP LEFT: On August 19, 1958, Canadian National 6200, a 16-year-old 4-8-4, works west with a scheduled passenger train at Sunnyside in Toronto, Ontario. *Richard J. Solomon*

ABOVE: Canadian National 4-8-4 6218 leads an excursion on Central Vermont across the Georgia high bridge south of St. Albans, Vermont. *Jim Shaughnessy*

LEFT: Canadian National Railways' streamlined northern 6404 was photographed on the ready track at Niagara Falls, Ontario, on November 1, 1958. *Ron Wright*

Pioneer Northerns

The 4-8-4 resulted from an expansion of the 4-8-2, but it was originally built to accommodate low-grade fuel. Only later was it refined into the ultimate eight-coupled type.

In the mid-1920s, Northern Pacific required a more effective Mountain type for heavy passenger trains but wanted to fuel it with locally mined, low-yield Rosebud coal. This was procured for roughly 70 percent less cost than that of high-energy eastern coal but suffered from high ash content and required a bigger firebox to burn effectively. In 1926 NP worked with Alco on the design, which resulted in a new type using a four-wheel trailing truck to support an unusually large firebox with its ungainly ashpans. A couple of years later, NP and Alco repeated this developmental exercise to create a massive freight hauler called the Yellowstone (see Chapter 5).

Although they were the first of the type, and reasonably successful in performing the job for which they were built, NP's pioneering 4-8-4s lacked the well-balanced design and handsome proportions that later came to typify the Northern type. Nevertheless, within a year of NP, three other lines adopted the 4-8-4.

Canadian National Railways had only recently pieced together a trans-Canadian network from the financial ruins of various private railway ventures. CN's predecessors had favored eight-coupled types, including the 2-8-0, 2-8-2, and 4-8-2, so a general-application 4-8-4 was a logical progression. CN began with an order for 40 locomotives, and over the next two decades the Canadian giant, along with its American subsidiary, Grand Trunk Western, assembled the largest North American 4-8-4 fleet: 203 locomotives. These were handsome, powerful, dual-service machines that enjoyed a comparatively light axle weight, which allowed them great route availability.

Some Western Achievers

The 4-8-4 type was especially popular with lines west of Chicago, where long runs and high speeds were the norm. The lines ordered a variety of excellent engines built with ample boilers and tall drivers for freight and passenger service. For all-around performance, many of the western 4-8-4s will be remembered as among the finest locomotives to have ever worked American rails. High boiler output combined with tall drivers meant that 4-8-4s were well suited for working heavy passenger trains, being able to both sprint across wide-open spaces in level country and to dig in and march up the prolonged climbs that defined western mountain railroading. All the big western roads adopted the type, and most bought them in comparatively large numbers.

Atchison, Topeka & Santa Fe, among the earliest to adopt the 4-8-4 type, bought them concurrently with 4-6-4s. Its first locomotives were of the 3751 class and built by Baldwin as coal burners; they were later rebuilt to burn oil. The pioneer example of this class, engine 3751, survives to the present; restored in the 1990s for excursion work, it has made occasional trips on its old home rails.

Santa Fe's finest Northerns were its 10 3776 class engines, built on the eve of World War II, and 30 2900 class engines, delivered during the war. These featured 80-inch drivers and 300 psi boiler pressure; they were famous for exceptional power and speed. Designed to operate continuously at 90 mph, they were known to have easily hit the 100-mph mark and were among the largest fast steam locomotives ever built. On level track, a lone Santa Fe 4-8-4 could easily race along with 15 traditional heavyweight passenger cars in tow.

Southern Pacific's Coast route from San Francisco to Los Angeles was among the great American railroad journeys; this

ABOVE: Santa Fe's late-build Baldwin 4-8-4s were among the finest in the land. Locomotive 3783 emits a clean exhaust as it leads long freight on one of Santa Fe's western mainlines in the early 1950s. *Robert A. Witbeck*

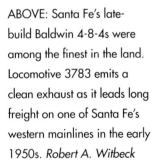

ABOVE RIGHT: One of Santa Fe's war babies, 2900-series 4-8-4 number 2919. By the time this locomotive was built, Santa Fe had already begun to dieselize freight operations with FTs. *Robert A. Witbeck*

was the original route for SP's famed *Daylights,* its glamorous art deco–styled red, orange, and silver streamliners.

When on March 21, 1937, Southern Pacific debuted its new streamlined *Daylights,* it simultaneously introduced its new Lima-built 4-8-4s. These were more than mere locomotives; they were elegant, streamlined masterpieces of engineering. Lima initially built SP six 4-8-4s, considered the most modern locomotives of their kind when delivered in late 1936 and early 1937. They were assigned class GS-2 (GS standing for "Golden State" or "general service") and numbered 4410–4415.

SP's *Daylight* service 4-8-4s were streamlined to fulfill aesthetic ideals. Unlike other streamlined engines that disguised machinery and the engine form with wind-resistant shrouds, SP's were "cleanlined" while maintaining a classic appearance. Boiler casing enclosed external piping and protrusions such as the sand domes, steam dome, exhaust stack, and

other unsightly equipment while the locomotive maintained its essential form. Reciprocating parts—drive rods, connecting rods, and valve gear—were highly polished alloy steel. The drive wheels were the modern cast-steel Boxpok style instead of the old-fashioned spoked variety. The angular pilot, decorated with rows of silver stripes emulating the appearance of the fabricated lattice-style pilot on older passenger locomotives, was intended to avoid interference with the front coupler and airline brake hoses.

Sheet-metal skirting ran on the sides of the boiler from the pilot to the cab. The locomotive headlight was located in centered streamlined housing on the smokebox door. The paint livery matched the *Daylight* train sets—the boiler casing was glossy black; the smokebox doors, marker lamps, horns, and other front-end equipment were painted aluminum; and the pilot and side skirting were painted brilliant shades of orange to mimic the California poppy, the state flower. A deep red

ABOVE LEFT: Photos of Southern Pacific's Lima-built 4-8-4s are common, but images, such as this one, that show the back of the tender are relatively rare. *Robert A. Witbeck*

ABOVE: Southern Pacific 4449 leads a created *Daylight* train at Algoma, Oregon, on June 24, 1984. *George W. Kowanski*

LEFT: The city of Portland, Oregon, holds title to Spokane, Portland & Seattle Class E-1 No. 700 and Southern Pacific Class GS-4 No. 4449. *Tom Kline*

BELOW: Jim Shaughnessy caught up with Union Pacific's first 4-8-4, engine 800, working eastbound near Lexington, Nebraska, on July 26, 1955. *Jim Shaughnessy*

RIGHT: Although largely a passenger locomotive, Union Pacific's 4-8-4s were well suited to fast freight work. Engine 800 leads an eastward freight at Lexington, Nebraska, on July 26, 1955. *Jim Shaughnessy*

stripe ran across the midsection of the boiler. The tender continued this striping pattern, which carried on throughout the streamlined passenger consist, giving the whole train a look of distinction and continuity.

The success of SP's *Daylight* led to more streamlined trains and more Lima 4-8-4s with further refinements to the design. In 1938, SP received 14 class GS-3s featuring many subtle improvements, including taller driver wheels. The finest of the lot were SPs 28 GS-4s built in 1941, numbered 4430–4457.

Lima featured its SP 4-8-4s in advertisements describing them as its latest batch of "Super-Power": "The Locomotives will be used to power the new 'Overnight' passenger trains that the Railroad had inaugurated between San Francisco and Los Angeles as well as the famous *Daylight* trains between the two cities. In addition to passenger service, these locomotives will also be used to power the overnight 'Hotshot' freight that the Southern Pacific has so successfully been using to reclaim LCL [less than carload] freight."

World War II placed great pressure on SP, and during the war it received its final 10 Lima 4-8-4s, classed GS-6s. These locomotives featured a more utilitarian appearance than the prewar engines as their construction was limited by War Production Board regulations on locomotive design and materials.

Union Pacific developed the 4-8-4 type a decade after Northern Pacific, but ultimately its 4-8-4s were viewed as among the finest of the type. In the late 1930s, UP worked with Alco in the design of a powerful Northern type with high drivers, following an approach similar to that adopted by the other western lines. In 1937, Alco delivered 20 UP 4-8-4s, Nos. 800–819 (UP class FEF-1, using a system that signified the wheel arrangement, four-eight-four). Among the qualities of their thoroughly modern design were one-piece cast-steel integral bed frames, Boxpok drivers, and Timken roller bearings on all axles. UP placed two repeat orders with Alco for improved 4-8-4s, delivered in 1939 and in 1944.

UP's 4-8-4s were fast, powerful engines designed to run at a sustained 90 mph hauling a 1,000-ton passenger train and counterbalanced for 110 mph. They are believed to have operated at 100 mph in service. Equally impressive was the engine's exceptional 93 percent service availability, which exceeded that of most steam power. However, like some Northern Pacific and Santa Fe top steam, UP's 800s regularly worked approximately 15,000 miles a month. UP 844 was the last of the lot, and the most famous because it was never retired and has continued to serve the railroad for which it was built.

Union Pacific had the wisdom and ample resources to make magic: on April 24, 1981, it operated this double-headed steam special with its ever-popular 4-8-4 8444 and recently restored Challenger 3985. *George W. Kowanski*

On June 28, 1986, a little more than four decades after Reading Company's Reading, Pennsylvania, shops outshopped T-1 2102, the restored locomotive poses at the old shops with former Gulf Mobile & Northern Pacific 425. *Chris Bost*

Modern Eight-Coupled Engines in Anthracite Country

After World War I, Lackawanna and Lehigh Valley developed long-distance bridge traffic and needed faster freight locomotives. These lines were among a half-dozen routes in the competitive New York City–Buffalo corridor, where New York Central's Water Level route had a natural advantage for the movement of freight.

In the mid-1920s, Lackawanna bought two fleets of 4-8-2s, one for road freight, the other for passenger service. Then, in 1927, the railroad emerged as one of the first to adopt the new 4-8-4 wheel arrangement. Its first batch were built by Alco and featured 77-inch wheels for passenger service. Considered to be the second group of 4-8-4s built in the

United States, the engines were called Poconos by Lackawanna rather than Northerns.

Lackawanna followed up with 20 more 4-8-4s with smaller drivers for fast freight work; more came in 1932, followed by 20 dual-service 4-8-4s with 74-inch drivers in 1934. Both of these orders were significant as they were placed when few American railroads were investing in new steam power.

Lehigh Valley also sampled Alco's three-cylinder 4-8-2s in the mid-1920s, having ordered some of the earliest examples of the type. In 1930, Lehigh Valley sampled 4-8-4 designs, buying one each from Alco and Baldwin. These became known as Wyomings (in reference to the significant Pennsylvania anthracite fields the railroad served), and following trials, they were deemed worthy for service. Lehigh Valley took an unusual move and ordered 10 each from Alco and Baldwin, bringing its fleet to 22 locomotives. As previously mentioned, Erie, which was among the competitors for New York–Buffalo traffic, assembled an impressive fleet of high-driver 2-8-4 Berkshires.

Among the last railroads in the region to make use of this versatile wheel arrangement was the Reading Company. In the nineteenth century, Philadelphia & Reading grew from the amalgamation of myriad eastern Pennsylvania anthracite haulers. While Lackawanna and Lehigh Valley expanded their lines to reach to Buffalo and Niagara Falls, Reading remained focused on its traditional geographic area. Although it had built connections far enough to interchange coal traffic, and later developed some bridge traffic, its lines never expanded much beyond eastern Pennsylvania and New Jersey.

Within this narrow geographical scope, Reading operated an unusually dense network characterized by multiple-track mainlines with complex signaling that hosted dense suburban passenger service and heavy freight traffic. Its freight lines crossed several difficult mountain grades, which included some of the steepest in the East.

Historically, Reading locomotives burned a variation of the hard anthracite the line was famous for hauling. Anthracite culm (or coal waste) was its choice of fuel because of its natural abundance. Anthracite's hard, slow-burning characteristics required a special type of locomotive firebox. Because the material took longer to ignite and burned slower and hotter, anthracite-burning locomotives required a broad, shallow firebox grate. Back in 1877, Philadelphia & Reading's general manager, John E. Wootten, had designed such a firebox, which provided ample area for the combustion of anthracite culm.

In many instances, the Wootten firebox was too wide to allow traditional placement of the engineer's cab at the back of the locomotive. Instead, the engineer's controls were situated toward the middle of the locomotive in a cramped, awkwardly placed cab that straddled the boiler while providing just a short exposed platform at the back of the locomotive for the fireman. This produced the characteristic humpback locomotive type known colloquially as either a Camelback or a Mother Hubbard. Not only were these engines common on the Reading, but they were widely used by most anthracite haulers, including Central Railroad of New Jersey, Delaware & Hudson, Erie, Lackawanna, Lehigh & Hudson River, Lehigh Valley, Lehigh & New England, and others.

Reading and other lines adapted the Wootten firebox for use on locomotives with a conventional cab arrangement as railroads moved away from burning straight anthracite culm in favor of anthracite blended with softer bituminous coal, as well as straight bituminous. For example, Lackawanna began the shift to bituminous coal for locomotive fuel before World War I with orders for 2-8-2 Mikados.

Reading initially ignored the 4-8-4 trend, and in the 1930s the railroad made the uncommon decision to invest in 2-10-2s with moderate-sized driving wheels. However, Reading remained loyal to steam locomotives longer than its neighbors; equally significantly, it continued to build and make heavy modifications to its steam power decades after most American roads turned to buying motive power commercially. As it turned out, Reading was among the final few American railroads to build many of its own engines, which placed it in a league with other important coal-hauling railroads including Baltimore & Ohio, Illinois Central, Norfolk & Western, and Pennsylvania Railroad. Reading's main shops, appropriately located at the railroad's Pennsylvania namesake (Reading, Pennsylvania) completed construction of more than 600 locomotives by the end of the steam era.

In 1945, Reading opted to meet traffic demands with a home-built 4-8-4 design that was best suited to its immediate freight requirements. So 18 years after that wheel arrangement had debuted on Northern Pacific, Lackawanna, and Santa Fe, Reading set out to assemble its own fleet of 4-8-4s. Steam locomotives are adaptable machines; rather than starting from scratch, Reading's shops reused boilers and fireboxes from the railroad's powerful class I-10sa 2-8-0 Consolidations as a foundation for the new class T-1 4-8-4. Reading's I-10sa had proven to be a powerful Consolidation and equaled the output of 2-8-2 Mikados on many lines, so its wide-diameter boiler was ideal for a larger locomotive. Reading lengthened I-10sa boilers and replaced the Consolidation's conventional drivers with taller modern Boxpok disc drivers.

Although not the most powerful, the fastest, or the most significant class 4-8-4s, Reading's 30 T-1s were comparable to Lackawanna and Lehigh's freight service 4-8-4s. And for more than a dozen years, these engines worked heavy freight on Reading's mainlines, hauling through freight and coal trains. But like many late-era steam locomotives, the T-1's freight career was cut short.

Despite its postwar investment in the T-1s, by the late 1940s, the Reading Company, like most other North American lines, was sold on the cost effectiveness of modern diesel power. The T-1s were only used in regular service for a little more than a half-dozen years. Despite rapid dieselization in the 1950s, they were kept for extra moves and peak traffic until spring 1956. In their last years, the T-1s worked a variety of assignments out of Shamokin, St. Clair, Tamaqua, and Gordon, Pennsylvania, both leading freights and serving as pushers. In early 1956, Reading loaned a half-dozen T-1s to the power-hungry Pennsylvania Railroad, which employed them for a short time on its Susquehanna Division.

Had Reading scrapped all 30 T-1s on the arrival of diesels, this class would have remained a relatively obscure application of the 4-8-4 type. As freight locomotives, they largely toiled in the background and away from the public eye. Only the most seasoned railway photographers had sought them out. However, this was not the case. After Reading concluded its regular steam operations in 1957, it retained five T-1s, and on October 25, 1959, the railroad reintroduced the type as a passenger excursion locomotive. Over the next five years, it hosted about four dozen Iron Horse Rambles with several of the surviving T-1s. These excursions covered much of Reading's complex network, carrying thousands of delighted railroad enthusiasts. After Reading's steam rambles concluded, four of the T-1s survived (engine 2123 was scrapped in Modena, Pennsylvania, in 1965).

In the 1970s, former Reading 2102 was painted red, white, and blue and was among the three steam locomotives used to haul the American Freedom Train, a commemorative train designed to celebrate the American bicentennial in 1976. The book isn't closed on the T-1 yet. Locomotive 2101 resides at the Baltimore & Ohio Railroad Museum in Baltimore, while 2124 is among the big steam on display at the Steamtown National Historic Site in Scranton, Pennsylvania. Locomotive 2100 has been more elusive. After years in storage in St. Thomas, Ontario, it was moved to Washington State and in April 2015 was sent to Ohio where it was expected to undergo operational restoration. Locomotive 2102, which worked Reading & Northern excursions in the 1980s and early 1990s, is stored on the railroad at Port Clinton, Pennsylvania, pending restoration to service.

OPPOSITE: In the late 1940s, Reading 2127 leads a coal train by ancient Hall disc signals. *John Pickett collection*

New York Central Niagara

In the mid-1940s, New York Central's locomotive genius Paul Kiefer remained unconvinced by the recent advances in diesel-electric technology. He worked with Alco to refine a super 4-8-4 for the railroad. The prototype 4-8-4, ready by August 1945, was intended for both high-speed passenger service and fast freight work. New York Central called it the Niagara type; it was the culmination of Kiefer's earlier work, blending elements of his 4-8-2 Mohawks and 4-6-4 Hudsons into a locomotive with superb performance capabilities.

Complicating the design was the need for the powerful locomotive to conform to New York Central's unusually restrictive loading gauge, which limited the locomotive machinery to a space just 10 feet 5 inches wide and 15 feet 3 inches tall. To create a larger boiler space within these confines, Kiefer took a creative tack. Among other novel decisions, he dispensed with the conventional steam dome and used a dry pipe for steam collection. His boiler design was considered one of the best despite its size constraints, and it proved to be substantially more productive than the boiler designs used by many other 4-8-4s. Consistent with New York Central's other modern steam power, the Niagara used a cast-steel integral bed frame, lightweight alloy-steel reciprocating parts with precision counterbalancing, and widespread application of Timken roller bearings.

Central ordered an additional 26 Niagaras during 1945 and 1946. In service, some of Central's Niagaras averaged more than 25,000 miles per month. However, while they matched modern diesel performance, they did so at greater cost, so their time in service was unusually brief. It was a sad case of perfecting steam technology too late in the race for superior overall efficiency and operational cost.

ABOVE: New York Central Niagara 6001 was only a few months old when it was photographed racing along the east shore the Hudson River near Breakneck Ridge north of Cold Spring, New York, on June 23, 1946. *Donald W. Furler*

OPPOSITE: New York Central's Niagara squeezed the most amount of boiler possible within the confines of the railroad's restrictive loading gauge. Niagara 6004 works west at milepost 252 west of Rome, New York. *Robert. A. Witbeck*

Ten-Coupled Steam Power: Decapods, Santa Fes, Overland, and Texas Types

BY VIRTUE OF THEIR MANY DRIVE WHEELS, 10-coupled locomotives seem synonymous with big twentieth-century power, even though the 10-coupled type was really a nineteenth-century innovation.

In the late 1860s, Lehigh Valley had ordered a pair of 2-10-0s from Norris that are believed to be the first of their type in the United States. Following some Baldwin-built exports in the mid-1880s, Northern Pacific ordered a similar type of 2-10-0, while in 1891, Erie Railroad bought some exceptionally large 2-10-0s for the period. These were Camelbacks and assigned as helpers east of Lanesboro, Pennsylvania, on the grade over Gulf Summit. However, owing to the necessity for a long wheelbase

and unusually high steam consumption, 10-coupled locomotives remained relatively obscure until after 1900.

Among the drawbacks of 10-coupled types was the need for tremendous piston thrust to move five sets of drive wheels and associated reciprocating parts, placing great stress on the frame and cylinders. Small wheels were difficult to counterbalance properly, and the locomotives tended to pound the tracks, which limited most 10-coupled types to comparatively

Decapod type as a mainline drag engine. Yet it perfected this wheel arrangement into a high-powered hauler, and between 1916 and 1924 the railroad acquired North America's largest fleet of 2-10-0s—598 nearly identical locomotives. It classified these as I1s (*s* for "superheated"), which is probably one of the most confusing designations of all time; to avoid problems think of the type as "eye one ess."

PRR's fleet represented the lion's share of the American 2-10-0 type built for domestic service. Alfred Bruce points out that while Baldwin and other builders exported many 2-10-0s, which was a very popular type overseas, there were only about 700 2-10-0s built for domestic applications. One of the most common varieties was an export type designed for service in Russia during World War I. When the Russian Revolution orphaned these engines, they found their way onto American lines.

In addition to PRR, Erie Railroad, St. Louis–San Francisco (the Frisco), Seaboard Air Line, and Western Maryland were among American lines that made good use of 2-10-0 types; except for WM's, these engines seemed small compared to PRR's big 2-10-0s. On most lines the 2-10-0 arrangement was generally known as the Decapod, but on PRR they earned the nickname "Hippos"—a descriptive term owing to their relatively small wheels, abnormally large boilers, and front-mounted dual air reservoirs. They were well suited to mountainous freight operations in PRR's Central Region east of Pittsburgh. They worked a variety of heavy duties, including coal service and as pushers. However, it is understood that the engines were unpopular with crews on PRR's Lines West, and so rarely saw service west of Pittsburgh.

All but one of the Hippos were scrapped after the end of steam. Number 4483 was stored for many years at Northumberland with PRR's other preserved steam

ABOVE: Western Maryland 2-10-0 leads an eastward coal train at Keystone, east of Meyersdale, Pennsylvania. *Donald W. Furler*

PREVIOUS PAGE: Pennsylvania Railroad I1s Decapod 4311 marches northward on the Elmira Branch in 1957. Time was running out for these heavy hauling behemoths. *Jim Shaughnessy*

slow speed applications. Also, since 10-coupled locomotives needed larger cylinders, they consumed steam more quickly than smaller locomotives; by working hard at higher speeds, conventional boiler capacity would be exhausted faster.

Big Decapods

By 1916, many railroads had embraced the articulated Mallet compound type for heavy drag freight service (see Chapter 5). Pennsylvania Railroad had a brief flirtation with these "double engines" but preferred conventionally designed engines that used just two cylinders without the complexity of compounding or articulation. By this time, a number of lines had adopted the 2-10-2 type for heavy work, so it might seem unusual that Pennsy opted to develop and mass produce the 2-10-0

ABOVE: Pennsylvania Railroad I1s 2-10-0 3445 waits for a signal at Sodus Point, New York, to shove cars forward onto the massive Lake Ontario coal docks. *Ron Wright*

ABOVE RIGHT: On August 16, 1956, a Pennsylvania I1s Decapod is switching cars at Sodus Point, New York. This made for a fascinating subject for teenaged photographer Ron Wright, who captured the moment for posterity. *Ron Wright*

RIGHT: The bark of exhaust punctuates the locomotive's slow progress as it nimbly shoves coal hoppers toward the Sodus Point Docks. Notice the "doghouse" shelter for the head-end brakeman atop the tender. *Ron Wright*

Hippos conquer the Horseshoe Curve. No location was more famous for steam action than Pennsylvania Railroad's sublimely scenic Horseshoe Curve west of Altoona. Here mighty I1s 2-10-0s are seen working as head-end power and pushers on a westward freight. *Robert A. Witbeck*

On May 4, 1957, Jim Shaughnessy made this fine portrait of an elderly Pennsylvania Railroad 2-10-0 at work hauling merchandise freight northbound near Troy, Pennsylvania. *Jim Shaughnessy*

locomotives, but decades ago it was separated from its brethren. Today, while most surviving PRR steam is displayed at the Railroad Museum of Pennsylvania at Strasburg, the last Hippo is stored in western New York near Buffalo.

Santa Fe Type

Santa Fe ordered 2-10-0s for helper service on Raton Pass, but in 1902, due to difficulties backing the big locomotives down the long grade from the summit, it adapted its engines by adding a rear pony truck to aid with reverse moves. This

created the first 2-10-2, known as the Santa Fe type. In their first decades, Santa Fe's fleet of Santa Fes represented the vast majority of engines of this type. The railroad had approximately 160 of them in service by 1912. Burlington adopted the type that year and ordered some impressive looking 2-10-2s with very large boilers for drag service that *Railway & Locomotive Engineering* called "the largest [engines] ever built with all the driving wheels coupled in one group."

Over the next dozen years, the 2-10-2 emerged as a popular type for heavy freight service among railroads across the

ABOVE: Santa Fe 2-10-2 3865 catches the sun at Summit, California, at the top of Cajon Pass on January 22, 1946. *John E. Pickett*

RIGHT: A pair of New Haven Railroad 2-10-2s on loan to New York, Ontario & Western lead a 42-car westbound freight at Woodridge, New York, on July 5, 1947. *Donald W. Furler*

country. The type offered enormous pulling power without the problems associated with articulated compound design. The tradeoff was the locomotive's long wheelbase and high piston thrust. To make the engines more flexible and better able to negotiate curves, some varieties incorporated novel features such as flangeless middle drivers and lateral-motion devices on some driving axles, which afforded a bit of play in what was otherwise a rigid wheelbase. While not fast locomotives, the 2-10-2s were generally faster than the plodding Mallet compounds.

In August 1914, *Railway & Locomotive Engineering* profiled Baltimore & Ohio's latest locomotive, a large Baldwin 2-10-2 type: "[this] makes an interesting development of the

ABOVE: On September 6, 1952, no less than 40 axles of steam power were required to lift a westward, 95-car, Baltimore & Ohio iron-ore extra up the east slope of Sand Patch. The head end is seen passing at Manilla, Pennsylvania. *Donald W. Furler*

LEFT: Minutes after the head end, a second pair of Baltimore & Ohio 2-10-2s work as the helpers behind the caboose on this westward iron-ore extra. *Donald W. Furler*

non-articulated locomotive . . . the tractive forces exceeds that of many Mallet articulated locomotives of the 2-6-6-2 type." Significantly, like many new engines of the period, it was equipped with the latest type of Schmidt superheater.

Most 2-10-2s enjoyed long lives largely unnoticed. Most Santa Fe types were not especially sexy machines as locomotives go. They lacked the elegance of passenger-service Pacifics, and they didn't have the horsepower afforded by later eight-coupled types, but they were powerful, and when it came to pulling they really got the job done. Many worked low-priority trains such as coal and ore drags or worked in helper services.

The Texas Type—Ten-Coupled Superpower

On the heels of Lima's resounding success with its 2-8-4 Berkshire prototype, the builder moved quickly to apply the Superpower concept to the 10-coupled type. In the mid-1920s, the 2-10-2 had been selling as a popular heavy freight locomotive, so the expansion to a 2-10-4 was a logical step forward as this would provide a locomotive with even greater tractive effort while keeping axle loading within acceptable limits on most lines.

LEFT: One of Pennsylvania's massive J-class Texas types works upgrade at the Horseshoe Curve. *Robert A. Witbeck*

OPPOSITE: In a stunning display of exhaust, Central Vermont Railway's first 2-10-4, engine 700, departs White River Junction on July 3, 1949, leading train 430, which consisted of 60 cars. *Donald W. Furler*

In 1925, before its first production 2-8-4s were delivered to the Boston & Albany, Lima built a 2-10-4 type for the Texas & Pacific. While it wasn't the very first application for this novel wheel arrangement—Santa Fe had built an experimental 2-10-4 locomotive in 1919—the type was named for the T&P and became accepted as the Texas type, which seemed fitting for a very large locomotive. Texas & Pacific's 2-10-4 looked like big A-1s, and at first glance they could be mistaken for a B&A Berkshire if one ever had run in Texas. Both engines had large-diameter boilers; a prominent, overhanging, high-mounted Elesco feedwater heater; the headlight centered on the smokebox; and a pair of shielded pumps above the pilot.

Advances in locomotive design enabled Lima to overcome earlier structural limitations associated with 10-coupled loco-motives. While early Texas types were more powerful that 2-10-0s and 2-10-2s, they weren't designed for much greater speed and still featured relatively small drivers. Further development of the 2-10-4 involved improved counterbalance and the refinement of lighter reciprocating parts, combined with improved structural integrity, to allow for a comparably fast freight locomotive. Unlike the slogging 2-10-2s of the World War I era, these later 2-10-4 Texas types could really roll!

In 1930, Chesapeake & Ohio bought 2-10-4s from Lima that reflected the recent design of improved Berkshires for the Erie and were the first Texas types with high-driving wheels. Taller wheels reduced the number of wheel rotations needed for speed, which lowered the destructive reciprocating forces that had been associated with a 10-coupled type operated at higher speeds.

Santa Fe bought massive Baldwin 2-10-4s with lots of superlative characteristics, even taller drive wheels (74 inches in diameter compared to C&O's 70 inches), which required the largest cylinders ever used by a single-expansion engine (30x34

inches). Furthermore, they had the greatest piston thrust of any engine ever built, an estimated 210,000 pounds.

Pennsylvania Railroad, which had assembled the largest fleet of Decapods, ultimately ended up with the largest fleet of 2-10-4s. While this might seem like a logical progression, in fact it was an anomaly for PRR's philosophy that they even adopted the 2-10-4 type, let alone bought more of them than any other line. If the company had followed its own direction, it is unlikely they would have embraced this type; instead it would have preferred its peculiar Duplex types over a straight 10-coupled design. PRR had unusual ideas when it came to motive power design and often ignored industry trends. It had essentially boycotted most of the technological improvements and complexity introduced since World War I and instead focused on refining its own designs in the 1920s.

PRR hadn't sampled any of the Alco three-cylinder types, nor had it expressed interest in Lima Superpower designs. When its competitors were buying Hudsons, it preferred Pacifics; where many railroads were buying Northerns, it opted for Mountains. While PRR had pioneered the single-expansion articulated type, by the time other railroads were embracing commercially produced single-expansion articulateds, it had long lost its interest in the type.

During the 1930s, PRR was obsessed with electrification. The wiring of its heavily traveled New York–Philadelphia–Washington route and lines west to Harrisburg had freed up hundreds of older steam locomotives. So with the exception of its experimental S1 Duplex, which was intended for high-speed passenger service, PRR had not taken delivery of new steam power since 1930, when its last M1a Mountain-type was delivered.

World War II changed many things in railroading. The combination of an extraordinary traffic surge produced by

OPPOSITE: George C. Corey made this powerful portrait of Central Vermont Railway 2-10-4 703 on October 14, 1951, at White River Junction, Vermont. "Big" is entirely relative to your frame of reference: CV's 2-10-4s were the biggest steam power in New England and the smallest examples of the Texas type. *George C. Corey*

wartime traffic and the War Production Board restrictions on locomotive development produced conditions that no railroad, not even the PRR, could have anticipated before the war. To keep things simple, the WPB discouraged innovation and limited individual railroads in their ability to follow unusual paths in locomotive acquisition. Existing designs were mandated over engineering new types. So in the mid-1940s, when PRR wanted to move forward on its plans for superpowerful freight Duplex locomotives (ultimately adopted after the war), the WPB urged it to take a more conservative path and work from an existing heavy freight locomotive design. So PRR adopted and then adapted C&O's Class T-1 2-10-4 of 1930 as the model for its new locomotive.

Despite PRR's reluctance to adopt an existing type, PRR's class J 2-10-4 was an excellent example of late-era steam power. Some steam authorities have deemed PRR's J as its finest steam locomotive. These engines performed well, moving heavy tonnage at high speeds on level track, and demonstrated incredible power moving upgrade at slow speed around the Horseshoe Curve west of Altoona.

Of the 125 built, 65 locomotives were class J1, while the remaining 60 were class J1a. The J1a featured cast-steel frames produced by General Steel Castings Corporation and were slightly heavier than the J1. Most of PRR's J class worked through the war hauling tonnage west from Altoona, only occasionally straying east along the Middle Division. Compared with the likes of PRR's I1s 2-10-0s, the Js had short lives. Most of the Texas types were out of service, while some of the old 2-10-0 Hippos continued to labor in the slow speed work for which they were designed.

Alco Three-Cylinder 4-10-2s

Among the more unusual yet functionally successful adaptations of the 10-coupled arrangement were two fleets of three-cylinder 4-10-2s built by Alco in the mid-1920s. These used the same principle of three-cylinder design described in Chapter 3. As previously discussed, the economic prosperity that swept America in the 1920s had encouraged the movement of faster freight. Southern Pacific had a special need for big power. It was faced with mountain grades everywhere it went, and it desired a new locomotive that could deliver greater power and work at faster speeds than either its existing 2-10-2s Decks or its unique fleets of ponderous cab-ahead Mallet types (see Chapter 5). So Alco designed a new type of locomotive with the 4-10-2 wheel arrangement that was in effect an expansion of the 2-10-2 type but required an extra lead axle to help support the additional weight of the middle cylinder. The type had an abnormally long wheelbase that required compensation from a specialized lateral-motion adjuster designed by James G. Blunt for the driving box on the lead set of driving wheels. *Railway Mechanical Engineer* explained that, from its inception, the 4-10-2 wheel arrangement was called the Southern Pacific type, although Union Pacific, which also bought a few 4-10-2s, preferred the term Overland type after its Overland Route, a busy east-west transcontinental mainline).

SP's 4-10-2 locomotives performed well in the 30–35 mph range and were viewed favorably when serving in graded territory. Initially, SP assigned the 4-10-2s to work its formidable Donner Pass crossing and its sinuous Siskiyou line to Oregon. UP ordered a single experimental three-cylinder 4-10-2 from Alco in 1925. While it ultimately bought nine more 4-10-2s—and largely assigned these to service on its heavily graded Los Angeles & Salt Lake Route—in 1926 it worked with Alco to further expand the arrangement to a 4-12-2 type (see Chapter 5).

Titans of the Rails

AMERICAN ARTICULATED STEAM POWER MACHINES were the biggest of the big—true titans of the rails, with the ability to apply tremendous power to the tracks. From the dawn of the articulated era, these massive engines tipped the scales. As articulated types were refined, they continued to set new records for length, weight, and power.

The Mallet Compound

In the early twentieth century, when American railroads were facing ever greater waves of traffic, some locomotive designers turned to European technology for ways to improve American engine design. One solution appeared in the form of an articulated engine. While not a new idea, it was imported and expanded on a grand scale to produce the world's largest locomotives.

In the 1880s, the Swiss inventor Anatole Mallet (pronounced Mal-lay) had patented an articulated compound locomotive that essentially placed two engines under a common boiler. These were largely applied to narrow gauge lines, which faced axle weight and lateral-clearance restrictions prohibiting the use of more conventionally designed large engines.

Leonor F. Loree served as president of the Baltimore & Ohio at the dawn of the new century. A man of ideas and action, he pushed for innovation when others sought more conventional solutions. While Loree was noted for implementing many physical improvements to B&O's infrastructure and contributing to the advancement of American signaling,

Locomotive 2400 wowed railroad men and the public alike. It weighed more than 167 tons, substantially more than the record-setting 2-10-0 tandem compound constructed for Santa Fe just two years earlier. Alco boasted that it was the "heaviest and most powerful locomotive ever built." The rear set of drivers were powered by high-pressure cylinders, which exhausted into the front, low-pressure cylinders. The boiler contained 436 fire tubes, each 21 feet long. The forward engine was carried on a hinged frame and supported the boiler using a sliding bearing surface while flexible steam pipes connected the cylinders. Significantly, the articulated arrangement provided this huge machine with much-needed flexibility on sharp curves. However, the lack of a front guiding truck limited the top speed of its forward operations.

Unlike many radical approaches to locomotive design that were soon disregarded despite rosy promises of delivering greater power, the new Mallet met expectations, and the Mallet compound gained rapid acceptance on American lines. Not only was this pioneer Mallet to work B&O rails for three decades, but over a 45-year period as Mallet design was refined, approximately 2,400 locomotives were built for service in the United States using this basic design, though with a variety of wheel arrangements.

Locomotive 2400 set a number of significant technological precedents: it established a twentieth-century practice of using Walschaerts outside valve gear (designed by Belgian engineer Egide Walschaerts decades earlier) and was an early successful application of power-reverse gear, which was gradually adopted as standard equipment on new locomotives.

MALLETS IN SERVICE

B&O tended to work 2400 as a rear-end helper on its famed Sand Patch grade west of Cumberland, Maryland. Mallets were

ABOVE: Western Maryland 0-6-6-0 952 was truly an antique when it was photographed shuffling cabooses around at Hagerstown on July 28, 1950. *George C. Corey*

PREVIOUS PAGE: Virginian operated some of the largest Mallet compounds ever built, enormous 2-10-10-2s with forward-engine low-pressure cylinders that measured 4 feet in diameter. *John E. Pickett collection*

he also empowered B&O's general superintendent of motive power, John. E. Muhlfeld, to advance locomotive design in ways never previously tried in the United States. Muhlfeld worked with Alco's Schenectady Works and adapted the Mallet articulated compound from an agile narrow-gauge light locomotive into a colossal monster for freight service.

The result was unlike anything built before, and by far the heaviest locomotive built to date. It featured a 0-6-6-0 wheel arrangement put in two complete sets of running gear under a common boiler, and it steered American locomotive design toward vastly more powerful types.

The prototype, B&O road number 2400, was completed in the spring of 1904 in time for public display at the Louisiana Purchase Exposition in St. Louis. It was officially named J. E. Muhlfeld, after its designer, but soon after it became known unofficially as Old Maude, after a popular comic-strip mule.

designed for relatively slow-speed service, and the addition of leading wheels and trailing trucks solved tracking problems encountered with the original 0-6-6-0 wheel arrangement. In the Mallet's incarnations, the nature of its articulation and piping for the forward engine did not facilitate fast operation, nor was speed an important requirement since drag freight rarely traveled more than 20 mph.

The primary applications for Mallets were in situations where railroads wanted to reduce the need for double heading on heavy trains. The Mallet offered a means of doubling power controlled by a single locomotive crew. The two most common Mallet wheel arrangements were the 2-6-6-2 and 2-8-8-2. Considering that the 2-6-0/4-6-0 and 2-8-0 types represented the most common freight locomotives, it is fairly obvious what railroads hoped to achieve with two sets of running gear under a common boiler.

On some railroads, locomotive designations or classification reflected this philosophy: Southern Pacific classified the 2-6-6-2 as MM for Mallet Mogul, and the 2-8-8-2 as MC for Mallet Consolidation. While Mallets were much heavier than

By the time this Milwaukee Road 2-6-6-2 was photographed at Tacoma, Washington, on July 10, 1950, it was a rare bird about to become all but extinct. *John E. Pickett collection*

The ultimate Mallet and the last of its kind was Norfolk & Western's 2-8-8-2 Y6b. Engine 2177 pushes at the back on an eastbound at Blueridge, Virginia, on August 31, 1957.
Ron Wright

nonarticulated types, their multitude of drivers distributed the weight and limited the maximum axle loading, keeping locomotive weight within established safety parameters.

One of the difficulties facing railroads in the first decades of the twentieth century was that as its motive power became significantly more powerful, the inherent frailty of the rolling stock became an ever more apparent limitation to operations. By 1910, locomotives had become so powerful that they could quite literally pull a train apart if the power wasn't used judiciously. Among the advantages of the Mallet was its comparatively gentle firebox draft owing to its two-stage exhaust. However, in some instances, locomotives were too powerful to be effectively used strictly as head-end power on freights, especially in graded territory where stresses on draft gear (couplers, drawbars, and related equipment) represented a key operational limitation.

In these situations, the biggest locomotives could be assigned as rear-end pushers, where concerns of draft-gear strain were less important. The introduction of improved car design and steel framing changed operations as they made the use of much heavier trains possible.

NORFOLK & WESTERN Y CLASS

Norfolk & Western continued to refine the Mallet Compound for more than two decades after most other lines had abandoned the type. The basis for its design was the United States Railroad Administration 2-8-8-2 (a type that dated to World War I). N&W continued to improve the design, and in 1936 introduced its class Y6, which featured all the attributes of a modern steam locomotive, including a high-capacity boiler, cast-steel bed frames, mechanical lubrication systems, precision counterbalancing, and roller bearings. N&W continued to improve on this type, and built its Y6B variations up until

1952, by which time they were the last new road steam constructed in America.

The Y6s were very reliable locomotives noted for averaging 6,000 miles a month in heavy freight service. While they normally operated at about 20–30 mph, the type was capable of 50 mph in regular service.

SINGLE-EXPANSION ARTICULATED ENGINES

The Mallet compound arrangement fell out of favor in the 1920s when newer, more efficient, and faster nonarticulated types were preferred for fast freights; by then, 2-10-2s were nearly as powerful as a Mallet, without the complexity of articulation.

About this time, Mallet arrangement was transformed into what came to be called the simple articulated locomotive, a

single-expansion type instead of a compound. The type is distinguished by two sets of high-pressure cylinders, with boiler steam fed directly to all cylinders. This gave the simple articulated locomotive enormous power, if not greater efficiency, and locomotives of this type required amply sized boilers.

Pennsylvania Railroad built an experimental single-expansion compound in 1912 that was deemed unsuccessful, but a decade later the idea was successfully re-explored. During the mid-1920s, the single-expansion articulated locomotive was developed into a series of ever larger types that ultimately resulted in the creation of the world's largest and most powerful locomotives. Where the compound articulated type was designed for plodding slow-speed drag service, the simple articulated was aimed at speeding the movement of freight, and from the beginning these types were designed for power and greater speed.

ABOVE: On July 26, 1955, John Pickett and his friends caught up with Southern Pacific AC8 4191 on the Modoc Line at Madeline, California. *John E. Pickett collection*

OPPOSITE: On August 31, 1941, Chesapeake & Ohio 2-8-8-2 class H-7A 1579 leads a westbound freight under clear skies at Clifton Forge, Virginia. *Donald W. Furler*

LEFT: On March 20, 1961, National Railways of Mexico 2-6-6-2 2033 blasts out of a tunnel with a northward freight at Barrientos, north of Mexico City. *John E. Pickett*

Chesapeake & Ohio was first to order a significant fleet of single-expansion 2-8-8-2 articulateds, buying them from Alco in 1923 and 1924 and later purchasing a group of similar machines from Baldwin in 1925. This arrangement originally was called the Chesapeake type, although the name was rarely used. Great Northern also bought some enormously powerful Baldwin 2-8-8-2 simples in 1925. In the late 1920s, a number of railroads were operating massive simple articulateds while many railroads converted older Mallets to simple operation.

In 1927, Denver & Rio Grande Western ordered a heavy single-expansion 2-8-8-2 type for road freights. These engines were more than 74 feet long and were considered the world's largest locomotives to date. *Railway Mechanical Engineer* noted in October 1927 that "this type of locomotive was selected because it was considered impossible to build a non-articulated locomotive that would handle the trains that the D&RGW desired to operate." These big locomotives were the next step toward an even larger new type.

A National Railways of Mexico 2-6-6-2 labors through heat and haze north of Mexico City on March 18, 1961. *Jim Shaughnessy*

LEFT: After spending half a day in Anniston, Alabama, for repairs, N&W 1218 waits for a signal in the middle of the night in 1987 to resume its inaugural run. *John Gruber*

ABOVE RIGHT: N&W 1218 gets underway at Birmingham on its inaugural run to Roanoke in 1987. *John Gruber*

OPPOSITE: On August 1, 1987, two of Norfolk & Western's most famous engines, A-class 1218 and J-class 611, work together on an eastbound excursion at Vickers, Virginia. *George W. Kowanski*

ABOVE: Norfolk & Western's A-class 2-6-6-4 1240 has been polished up for an excursion at Bluefield, West Virginia, on July 11, 1959. *Richard J. Solomon*

LEFT: Although Rio Grande had originally bought the 2-8-8-2 single-expansion engines to lead freights, by 1952, the railroad had reassigned some of them to helper services. Rio Grande 3618 is at Tabernash, Colorado, waiting to push an eastbound to the Moffat Tunnel. *Robert A. Witbeck*

OPPOSITE: This rare photograph of Rio Grande 2-8-8-2 3618 working as a pusher on an eastward freight captures the scale of the machine against a panorama of the Colorado Rockies near Fraser. *Robert A. Witbeck*

BELOW: Rio Grande 3618 has completed its shove from Tabernash; the caboose of the eastbound freight is at the right. The train has entered the west portal of Colorado's Moffat Tunnel, a bore a little more than 6 miles long beneath the Rockies, which are immediately behind the photographer. *Robert A. Witbeck*

RIGHT: A locomotive engineer in the classic pose: hand on the throttle and eyes forward. He looks down the long length of the boiler on Rio Grande 2-8-8-2 3618 as it prepares to push an eastward freight toward Colorado's Moffat Tunnel. *Robert A. Witbeck*

When completed in 1928, the pioneer Northern Pacific 2-8-8-4 Yellowstone was the world's largest locomotive. Though the prototype was an Alco, subsequent locomotives, including this one, were built by Baldwin.
John E. Pickett

Yellowstones

In 1928, Northern Pacific was the latest to order what would become the next "world's largest locomotive." Big steam was NP's most cost-effective alternative for a difficult traffic problem and proved cheaper than rebuilding and relocating its difficult Yellowstone Division, which ran east from Glendive, Montana, across the Badlands to Mandan, North Dakota.

Further west, NP faced sustained mountain grades in excess of 2 percent. While the Yellowstone Division had a maximum gradient of only slightly more than 1 percent, its operations were complicated by a difficult sawtooth profile (the term stems from the comparison between the paper graph of the railroad grade and a saw blade). Further, a series of summits presented a special operating problem.

Steam operation on steep sustained grades was easily solved by assigning pushers to the difficult sections. Using helpers on Yellowstone district was complicated by the great length of the run, combined with the series of up-and-down grades.

Previously, NP had addressed the problem by halving the tonnage of mainline freights, keeping trains to a conservative 2,000 tons, but as traffic increased, this policy tended to clog up the mainline and increase operating expenses.

There were other considerations facing the railroad. As in the case of its pioneering development of the 4-8-4 (see Chapter 3), NP wanted to avoid importing high-quality coal from distant mines, desiring instead to burn locally mined Rosebud coal, a subbituminous lignite with poor heating value and high ash content. Not only did Rosebud coal require a larger grate to allow the boiler to supply ample volumes of steam, but NP also suffered from poor water along the line that tended to foam excessively in locomotive boilers.

NP worked with Alco, which delivered the experimental 2-8-8-4, engine number 5000, in 1928. This machine weighed nearly 360 tons fully serviced. Especially impressive was its vast firebox (more than 22 feet long and 9 feet wide), the largest ever conceived. Together, boiler and firebox used more than 5,000 stay bolts (a specialized bolt used to hold boiler plate together).

To demonstrate this capacious furnace, Alco staged a catered banquet for a dozen people inside it (before the locomotive was complete). It was the first conventionally oriented articulated type using a four-wheel radial trailing truck. Alco based the 2-8-8-4's design on Denver & Rio Grande Western's successful single-expansion 2-8-8-2 (described above) but required a twin-axle trailing truck to support the heavier firebox. Northern Pacific named the new locomotive wheel arrangement in honor of its Yellowstone District and classified the type as its Z-5.

Tests with the prototype produced mixed results. The 2-8-8-4 is understood to have suffered from steam leaks and some minor mechanical problems. Ultimately NP ordered 11 more Yellowstones, but they weren't from Alco. It awarded the remaining production entirely to Baldwin, Alco's chief competitor. While railroads often split orders between manufacturers, it was unusual to abandon a builder after they'd built a prototype and not reward them with at least a portion of the production order.

The locomotives proved adequate for the service required of them, and they labored in relative obscurity across the windswept Badlands. Working hard, they could burn up to 20 tons

The cab-forward articulated was one of the most distinctive locomotive arrangements and unique to Southern Pacific. SP cab-forward class AC-8 4185 is seen on its descent of Donner Pass in the early 1950s. *Robert A. Witbeck*

ABOVE: Duluth, Missabe & Iron Range's Yellowstone 222 marches along at speed on July 5, 1960. The long string of low-profile ore "jennies" (as ore cars are known) makes the enormous locomotive seem even larger. *Ron Wright*

OPPOSITE: July 5, 1960, was the day of destiny for steam-powered freight on Duluth, Missabe & Iron Range. A track gang gives a final salute as Yellowstone 222 roars northward with empties. Somewhere, not too far away, young Robert Zimmerman tunes his guitar. *Ron Wright*

of lignite an hour. In later years, NP transferred the locomotives west and largely used them as helpers.

In the early 1950s, John Pickett was visiting Northern Pacific's Livingston, Montana, engine terminal, where the railroad based its helpers for the westward shove over Bozeman Pass. "A friendly crew invited me into the cab of one of those Yellowstones. I looked into the firebox and it was like a vision of hell—fire and brimstone."

MORE YELLOWSTONES

Beginning in 1928, Southern Pacific made good use of the essential Yellowstone wheel arrangement but in reverse, as standard single-expansion cab-forwards that had four-wheel leading trucks operating firebox first, technically making them 4-8-8-2s. The cab-forward articulated arrangement dated to 1912, when SP reversed the orientation of its oil-fired Mallets for service on Donner Pass. This was a function of the need to work articulated locomotives at high altitudes through snowsheds

Southern Pacific AC-9 3809 works a westbound extra freight near Vaughn, New Mexico, on February 22, 1953. Most of the cars are empty refrigerator cars.
Robert A. Witbeck

and tunnels where crews were at risk of asphyxiation from exhaust gases. From 1928 to 1944, it placed successive orders with Baldwin for simple articulateds of the cab-forward type.

Not all of SP's lines were plagued with tunnels nor blessed with ready supplies of oil for fuel. Its Rio Grande Division—the famed Golden State Route running northeasterly from El Paso, Texas, toward Tucumcari, New Mexico—was wide-open country and had not a tunnel on the line. SP serviced New

Mexico's Dawson coalfields, which supplied the railroad with ample quantities of cheap, low-grade, bituminous coal.

Lima's excellent 4-8-4s, which were built for *Daylight* passenger trains, encouraged SP to work with the builder for a conventionally oriented articulated for fast freight work east of El Paso. And SP's "cab-behind" single-expansion articulateds were Lima's first modern articulated locomotive type. The first of 12 was shipped in the fall of 1939. These machines spent the next 13 years working as intended, hauling freights on the largely single-track Rio Grande Division. They were respected for their excellent service and unusually good looks. While originally coal burners, in 1950 they were converted to oil.

During World War II, Duluth, Missabe & Iron Range was pressed for power as its principal commodity—iron ore—was in record demand. DM&IR moved ore in some of the nation's heaviest trains from mines in northern Minnesota to docks on Lake Superior at Duluth and Superior, Wisconsin, where the ore was transloaded to Great Lakes ships for onward movement to steel-producing centers in Indiana, Ohio, and

Pennsylvania. In 1943, the War Production Board granted authority to Baldwin to build 19 Yellowstones for Iron Range service. Although proportionally similar to NP's titans, they burned higher grades of coal and thus had smaller fireboxes.

Challengers

In the mid-1930s, Union Pacific worked with Alco to develop a fast and very powerful articulated engine. The 4-6-6-4 type was created to make a more flexible locomotive powered by 12 driving wheels rather than the three-cylinder 4-12-2 type Alco had built for UP between 1926 and 1930. The 4-12-2

Union Pacific 3985 was eastbound at Green River, Wyoming, on June 28, 1982. One of two surviving 4-6-6-4s, UP returned this giant to service in 1981. *George W. Kowanski*

OPPOSITE AND LEFT: Coming-and-going views portray a pair of Northern Pacific class Z-6 Challengers working a heavy freight in the rolling Palouse country west of Pasco, Washington, in 1955. *John E. Pickett*

offered great power but faced limited applications because of its unusually long wheelbase. By contrast, the new 4-6-6-4 combined a variety of technological advances with existing designs to make for a remarkably versatile big locomotive.

The new arrangement was called the Challenger type. Its four-wheel leading truck improved front-end stability and helped distribute weight between the forward and rear engines, which made for a more balanced overall design. A well-engineered suspension aided operation at higher speeds. Notably, the new arrangement also featured much-improved articulated connections. Typical of large single-expansion articulated types, the Challenger had a high-capacity firebox and large-diameter boiler, but it also had relatively tall drivers to allow for a top running speed of 80 mph. The Challenger worked both freight and passenger trains.

Alco delivered the first 4-6-6-4 articulateds to UP in 1936. Ultimately the railroad ordered 105 of the type from Alco. Beginning about 1940, Alco improved on its earlier design by further refining the method of articulation using a cleverly designed lateral bearing surface that supported the forward engine, minimized vertical movement, and improved ride quality. This was a significant improvement, which Bruce described in *The Steam Locomotive in America* as "the most stable-riding articulated engine ever built."

The 4-12-2 type had been unique to Union Pacific, but the Challenger was built for many different railroads. More than 250 were produced, making it the most numerous single-expansion articulated type in the United States. Most Challengers were built by Alco, including those for Clinchfield, Delaware & Hudson, Northern Pacific, Rio Grande, Spokane,

OPPOSITE: On July 12, 1952, Delaware & Hudson Challengers work freight toward Ararat summit. Engine 1532 is in the lead with 1520 pushing at the back. *Donald W. Furler*

The syncopated bark of Challengers fore and aft on this southward freight could be heard for miles around. D&H's Challenger era was short and sweet. Some of these locomotives worked for less than a decade. *Donald W. Furler*

Portland & Seattle, and Western Pacific. Baldwin also built 4-6-6-4s for Rio Grande and Western Maryland.

An all-around excellent locomotive, the Challenger suffered from its late-era development: It was born during the Great Depression on the eve of the introduction of commercially built freight diesels. In the 1940s, the type was competing with diesels for market share, so the 4-6-6-4 fleets had comparatively short lives. Delaware & Hudson bought 40 from Alco, with the last locomotives delivered in 1946, but completely converted to diesel operations using Alco road-switchers by 1953; some of its Challengers were only in service for little more than a half-dozen years before being sent for scrap.

In practice, Challengers mostly worked in road freight service. Photographs of them leading passenger trains are rare, with the obvious exception of Union Pacific's famed 3985 (one of two preserved Challengers), which was restored for excursion service in 1981 and has been widely operated by the railroad in the last three decades.

RIGHT: Western Maryland Challenger 1208 leads westward freight WM-1 4 miles west of Cumberland, Maryland, and is about to enter the famed Helmstedder's Curve. *George C. Corey*

OPPOSITE: Moving freight over Ararat Summit demanded some of the heaviest applications of motive power in the East—no less than four locomotives were working this 108-car train at Forest City, Pennsylvania. *Donald W. Furler*

LEFT: On June 7, 1952, Western Maryland Challenger 1203 shoves at the back of priority freight WM-3 working west of Cumberland, Maryland, at Helmstedder's Curve. *George C. Corey*

Low sunlight finds Union Pacific Big Boy 4010 at rest in the early 1950s. Many photographers made the pilgrimage to Wyoming to see these engines under steam. *Robert A. Witbeck*

BIG BOY

Lucius Beebe was among period authors in starstruck awe at Union Pacific's Big Boy. He described it in his book *Trains in Transition*, noting that "its boiler delivers 7,000 horsepower, it has a cruising speed of eighty miles an hour and consumes twelve tons of coal and 15,000 gallons of water every sixty minutes." Even if he didn't get the details quite right, you can

hear his words resonate in the tone of a classic radio announcer of the time. You didn't need to experience a Big Boy passing by you to know it was really huge in every respect.

But was it the biggest? When a million pounds of animated steel whirl past you with a mile or more of tonnage in tow, you're unlikely to look for details about its size. But, after the fact, you might want to know just how big it was.

The Big Boy was an expansion of the basic design of UP's successful Challenger. It was conceived in the shadow of the diesel, and not just any diesel, but Electro-Motive's famed model FT four-unit, 5,400 horsepower, streamlined freight diesel. In 1939, the FT made its debut barnstorming around the United States, demonstrating that diesel-electric technology could finally rival steam power as an efficient commercial freight service.

During the 1930s, General Motors, through its subsidiary Electro-Motive Corporation (renamed Electro-Motive Division in 1940), had built on a series of technological successes that demonstrated the capabilities of diesel-electric power. When by 1938 it was in the business of selling diesel-electric switchers and streamlined passenger diesels before the FT, no commercially available diesel could come close to modern steam in heavy freight service.

Today we can look back at history without surprise. Could anyone have ever doubted the superiority of the diesel? The FT demonstrated that the diesel was the future for American railroads, and ultimately this machine and its successors purged steam from the rails—save for excursions and publicity runs. But that didn't mean that everyone in the steam business simply gave up when the FT threatened steam locomotives' longstanding superiority. The FT didn't kill steam right away. Quite the contrary—it was like the grain of sand in the oyster's shell. It spurred construction of some extremely impressive steam locomotives.

Steam locomotive design had a long tradition of custom-tailoring locomotives to their specific intended operation. This was especially true for unusually large or extraordinarily fast engines, where the machinery was necessarily optimized for the limits of an individual railroad's infrastructure and intended applications.

In contrast, Union Pacific's transcontinental mainline across Wyoming was remarkably free from the restrictions that limited engine size on other railroads. Out on the wide-open, windswept plains, UP wanted an engine that could really pull. Of the few restrictions it faced was in its ability to turn and repair locomotives, and like other exceptionally large engines, the Big Boy was not built for a universal application. The lack of servicing and turning facilities large enough for the Big Boy at most Union Pacific terminals meant that these locomotives were not intended to roam far and wide but rather to fulfill the immediate requirements for which they were designed.

In July 1955, dinosaurs still roamed west of Cheyenne: Union Pacific Big Boy 4004 leads a westward freight through the rock cut east of Dale Creek Junction. *Jim Shaughnessy*

ABOVE: On the evening of August 16, 1957, Union Pacific 4-8-8-4 4017 simmers between assignments in the darkness at Laramie, Wyoming. *Jim Shaughnessy*

LEFT: Rolling thunder—Union Pacific works on Sherman Hill west of the Hermosa Tunnel on August 20, 1957. *Jim Shaughnessy*

In 1940, UP received high-priority heavy perishable trains from Southern Pacific at Ogden, Utah, and expedited them eastward over its graded transcontinental route over the Wasatch Range and across the high plains to Cheyenne, Wyoming. UP's Wasatch grades were by no means the steepest in the West, nor even the biggest impediment to UP's transcontinental operations, but these grades did pose operational difficulties and tended to clog up the railroad.

Perishable trains, sometimes called fruit blocks, were solid consists of agricultural produce that originated in California and other western states for transport to eastern and midwestern markets. They were among UP's fastest and most tightly scheduled freight moves; if produce was delayed too long, it would arrive rotten and be of no value to anyone.

Union Pacific was no stranger to the diesel; in fact it was among the diesel pioneers and had helped forward internal-combustion technology since before World War I. During the mid-1930s, UP embraced diesel power and worked with General Motors in the development of lightweight passenger trains. However, while it viewed diesel power as a tool for fast passenger work, it also had an excellent relationship with Alco resulting in the design of most of that manufacturer's most

In 2014, the biggest news in railroad preservation was Union Pacific's movement of Big Boy 4014 from Pomona in Southern California to its steam shop at Cheyenne, Wyoming, in preparation for restoration to service.
John Gruber

successful steam locomotives, including its three-cylinder 4-12-2s, the 800-class 4-8-4s, and the 4-6-6-4 Challengers illustrated in these pages.

Why didn't UP simply order FTs? A variety of factors influenced UP's desire to push steam design. The immediate cost of new diesels versus steam was undoubtedly a consideration. Diesels ultimately offered greater efficiencies, lowered the cost of labor, and reduced the number of locomotives required to move trains, but in 1940 a limited application, such as that proposed for the Big Boy, likely favored continued steam operation over the cost of diesel implementation.

Futhermore, steam had a long track record. While diesels would eventually demonstrate very high availability (a gauge of when locomotives are available to work), the FT represented technology in its infancy, and its long-term prospects were basically unknown. Today, with the benefit of hindsight, we know that the FT was vastly superior to the streamlined power cars of a few years earlier, but that wasn't necessarily assured at the time. And there were few railroads more familiar with the failings of early diesels than the Union Pacific. After more than five years of experience with the streamliners, UP's motive power chiefs were well aware of how well the early diesels performed in a real-world environment.

Lastly, steam-era machismo was at stake. You can just imagine an official at Union Pacific's offices in Omaha taunting his counterpart at Alco, suggesting that Electro-Motive's diesel was offering 5,400 drawbar horsepower and wondering if maybe Alco could do better than that with steam. UP ordered 20 4-8-8-4s from Alco in 1940, while Electro-Motive's expensive brown-and-yellow toy was roaming North American rails demonstrating the inadequacies of the 2-8-2 Mikado. UP followed with an order for another five during World War II. But after the war, all bets were off.

Trains & Travel editor David P. Morgan related the story of the type's famous name in the magazine's August 1952 issue, describing the prophetic actions of an Alco shop employee who was understood to have scrawled "Big Boy" in chalk on the smokebox door of a 4-8-8-4 under construction. The distinctive name stuck and brought fame to the massive machines. One wonders: had Union Pacific called them the Wasatch type as originally suggested, would the 4-8-8-4 have been as well known?

The 4-8-8-4 was impressive as a result of its exceptional length and weight. Complete with its tender, it was 132 feet 9 3/8 inches long, yet its articulated design enabled it to accommodate curves as tight as 20 degrees. Its engine weight alone was officially 386 tons, more than 17 times the weight of the original heavy mountain locomotive, Whistler's 0-8-0 Mud Diggers, built by Ross Winans of Baltimore a century earlier.

Sometimes the truth of the matter is very different from common perception. While Big Boy may have briefly held the title of world's heaviest steam locomotive, as it turns out Chesapeake & Ohio's massive 2-6-6-6 Alleghanies, built by Lima starting in 1941, were slightly heavier. This fact was obscured for decades and unknown during the steam era. It was finally revealed in the pages of *Trains* magazine in 1998 that while at the time of delivery C&O's Allegheny was officially listed as weighing slightly less than the Big Boy, this was due to a deliberate oversight. The true weight for the Allegheny was 775,330 pounds, slightly more than Big Boy's published weight of 772,000 pounds. But if one figure was fiddled over the years, is it not possible that other official figures were adjusted as well?

The Big Boys survived a few years longer than steam in other parts of the United States; they could be seen hauling trains over Sherman Hill west of Cheyenne as late as 1958. After the end of steam operations, almost one-third of the Big

Boy's total production was preserved. There are eight extant Big Boys today. In 2014, Union Pacific made news when it moved engine 4014 from Pomona, California, where it had been displayed, to Cheyenne, Wyoming, in preparation for its return to service as the world's ultimate steam excursion engine.

Appalachian Monsters

As noted above, in 1942 Chesapeake & Ohio tipped the scales one last time with an order for a ground-shaking 2-6-6-6 type

known as the Allegheny. C&O took delivery of the first locomotive in 1941, and ultimately Lima built 60 Alleghanies for C&O, with the last engine delivered in 1948. In 1945, it delivered eight to Virginian, which assigned them to haul some enormously heavy coal trains to its Hampton Roads coal port at Sewell's Point, Virginia.

Why buy a diesel if you can have these really fine steam locomotives? Baltimore & Ohio was among General Motor's earliest diesel customers. When B&O tested the FT, it was sold

Virginian 2-6-6-6 903 works an eastward freight at Norfolk, Virginia, on June 28, 1952. Patterned after Chesapeake & Ohio's 2-6-6-6 Allegheny, Virginian's eight class-AG 2-6-6-6s were among the world's largest engines. *John E. Pickett*

OPPOSITE: Ten percent of the EM-1 roster can be seen darkening the sky in northeastern Ohio as they work a heavily loaded coal train destined for the Lake Erie port at Fairport. *J. William Vigrass*

on the concept. However, World War II interfered with B&O's early dieselization. As with lines all across the continent, its traffic soared during the war. B&O wanted more FT diesels to fill the gap, but the War Production Board compelled B&O to purchase modern steam instead of additional FTs. The result was B&O's famous 2-8-8-4 EM-1s, all 30 of which were built by Baldwin. They were a compact Yellowstone type and one of the finest locomotives to work B&O rails. Originally assigned to mainline freights working west from Cumberland, Maryland, in later years they worked a variety of lesser duties, including coal drags on the branch to Fairport, Ohio.

RIGHT: Baltimore & Ohio's class EM-1s were handsome machines born of a need for wartime power. If B&O had a choice, they would have bought Electro-Motive FT diesels, but the War Production Board mandated steam. *J. William Vigrass*

Captions

PAGE 7: Export coal kept Norfolk & Western's mainline east of Roanoke busy in the mid-1950s. Heavy coal trains worked east from West Virginia mines toward N&W's tidewater port at Lamberts Point, Virginia. Helpers were required east of Roanoke to assist trains on the climb over the Blue Ridge. It was the last big steam show in the East. N&W refrained from buying diesels until the mid-1950s, and its massive A-class simple articulateds and Y-Class Mallets continued to work until 1960, several years after most eastern lines had completely dieselized. *Jim Shaughnessy*

PAGE 11: Engineer Ned Sutton was at the throttle of Lehigh & Hudson River (L&HR) No. 80. This was one of four USRA-designed 2-8-2 Mikados Baldwin built for the railroad in 1918, and featured 63-inch drivers. L&HR was an unusual railroad. It primarily served as a bridge carrier between the Maybrook, New York, yard at the west end of the New Haven Railroad and anthracite lines serving western New Jersey and eastern Pennsylvania around Easton and Bethlehem. Almost all of its locomotives were built for road service. The 2-8-0 Consolidation was its primary freight type, and although it bought two batches of four 2-8-2 Mikados in 1916 and 1918, in the 1920s it made the unusual move of returning to the 2-8-0 and bought some exceptionally powerful examples of the type. Its final steam locomotives were three 4-8-2 Mountains built by Baldwin in 1944 and patterned after Boston & Maine's class R-1 Mountains. *Donald W. Furler*

PAGE 12: On September 15, 1946, Lehigh Valley 4-8-4 5100 leads westward freight symbol JK1 with 66 cars at Triechlers, Pennsylvania. This was one of 22 4-8-4s Lehigh Valley ordered during the dark years of the Great Depression. In 1931, Alco and Baldwin each built a 4-8-4 for Lehigh Valley, and in 1932 the railroad graciously ordered 10 locomotives from each builder. While not a huge order, it was significant because so few locomotives were built as a result of the precipitous decline of railroad traffic. Baldwin's chief, Samuel Vauclain, sent a personal letter of thanks to Lehigh Valley for their business. *Donald W. Furler*

PAGE 13: When John E. Pickett captured this dramatic image of Santa Fe's Baldwin-built 2-8-2 Mikado 3225 in August 1952, the engine had been in service for more than three decades and would soon be replaced by diesels. The 2-8-2 Mikado type was one of the most common types of freight locomotive for many years, with nearly 10,000 of the type built for service in the United States. Although Santa Fe is famous for its handsome 4-8-4s and exceptionally powerful 2-10-4 Texas types, its common workhorse 2-8-2s were also worthy of a photographer's interest. *John E. Pickett*

PAGE 14: Canadian National Railways (CN) class U-2-e 4-8-4 6218 was a war child, built by Alco's Canadian affiliate, Montreal Locomotive Works, in September 1942. Its 73-inch drivers were typical of CN's 4-8-4 fleet, which worked freight and passenger traffic. The locomotive was preserved after the end of revenue steam, and following its eight-year stint in excursion service, it was retired to static display at Fort Erie, Ontario, opposite the Niagara River from Buffalo, New York. Sadly the once-handsome locomotive is reported to be in poor condition. *Richard Jay Solomon*

PAGE 15: Reading's T-1s were home-built locomotives that the railroad had rebuilt at its Reading, Pennsylvania, shops between 1945 and 1947 using the boilers of 2-8-0 Consolidations. After the end of its revenue steam in 1957, Reading Company retained five of its class T-1 4-8-4s, and from 1959 to 1964, these former freight engines entertained legions of loyal fans. Although steam had only been gone from the rails for a few years, nostalgia for the old order brought people out in droves. *Richard J. Solomon*

PAGE 15: The diesel-electric locomotive offered a more reliable and lower-cost motive power solutions for American railroads than even the finest modern steam power. The low cost of diesel fuel and high availability of diesel locomotives, combined with its great versatility and relative low maintenance costs, gave the diesel engine many advantages over steam. Between the end of World War II and 1960, mainline steam operations in the United States and Canada were phased out in favor of mass-produced diesel electric power. Yet nostalgia for the old order resulted in the preservation of a large number of steam locomotives. Some of these have been variously restored to working order. Engine 2012 was a star of Reading's Iron Horse Rambles in the 1950s and 1960s, and in the 1980s and early 1990s it was reactivated for excursion work on Blue Mountain & Reading/Reading & Northern, a Conrail-era regional spin-off that operates significant portions of the old Reading Company trackage in eastern Pennsylvania. *Chris Bost*

PAGE 16: Reading Company 2102 was one of 30 T-1 class 4-8-4s built by the railroad at its Reading, Pennsylvania, shops between 1945 and 1947, and one of three surviving examples of the type today. As of 2015, it was owned by the Reading & Northern, which aims to restore the locomotive for excursion service. Reading & Northern operates a network of trackage in the anthracite region of eastern Pennsylvania that is centered on former Reading Company lines acquired from Conrail in the 1980s and 1990s and also includes routes inherited from Central Railroad of New Jersey, Lehigh Valley, and Pennsylvania Railroad. *Donald W. Furler*

PAGES 16–17: Milwaukee Road 261, a powerful Northern-type steam locomotive built by Alco in 1944, exemplified modern steam locomotive practice, with Boxpok drivers, lightweight reciprocating parts, roller bearings on all axles, and a large high-capacity boiler. It was ordered during World War II when the War Production Board limited diesel construction in order to channel limited resources into the construction of military hardware while encouraging railroads to acquire new steam power of proven designs. If World War II hadn't occurred, many railroads might have begun dieselizing earlier instead of buying their final late-era steam power. *Brian Solomon*

PAGE 18: Union Pacific received 25 massive 4-8-8-4 Big Boy locomotives from Alco in two orders in 1941 and 1944. On July 25, 1955, engine 4004 from the 1941 order works west of Cheyenne, Wyoming, across that famous cleft in the high plains known on the railroad as Sherman Hill. The Big Boy was one of the largest reciprocating locomotives ever built, and the entire class spent most of their working lives on the windswept terrain between Cheyenne and Ogden, Utah, far from the populated areas of the United States. These large locomotive were very capable of moving long freight trains over great distances. *Jim Shaughnessy*

PAGE 19: Sadly, none of Erie's 2-8-4s survived the diesel invasion. So to the delight of photographers, a handsome Lima Berkshire was on Erie rails once again, more than three decades after the end of revenue steam operations. Unlike Erie, the Nickel Plate Road was generous in its preservation of steam locomotives, and several of its handsome Berkshires survive. *George W. Kowanski*

PAGE 19: Nickel Plate Road continued to buy new steam power for road freight service later than most railroads in the East. Lima's last order for new steam power was for 10 Nickel Plate Road 2-8-4s (class S-3) built in 1949. The railroad's late operation of steam and its early move into intermodal freight resulted in an unusual overlap of technologies. Scenes such as this one, with steam hauling piggyback trailers, were not uncommon on this railroad but were virtually unheard of on most North American lines, many of which didn't adopt piggyback until after diesels took over. *Jim Shaughnessy*

PAGE 20: Erie Railroad operated the largest fleet of Berkshires, totaling 105 locomotives. Its class S-3s were built by Baldwin and numbered 3350 to 3384, the last of which is pictured here working freight at Allendale, New Jersey. In its day, Erie Railroad was a heavy freight carrier, and it kept its 2-8-4s busy for more than 20 years. Unlike its competitors (Delaware, Lackawanna & Western; Lehigh Valley; and New York Central), Erie never ordered 4-8-4 Northern types. *Donald W. Furler*

PAGE 21: Photographer George C. Corey tells the story of this photo he exposed on December 7, 1941: "Sunday afternoon, a couple of days after my 17th birthday, seemed like a good time to get out of the house; my older sister had had a disagreement with our parents that threatened to escalate, so I hopped on my bike (the pedal variety) and headed down to the depot to hang out with the crossing tender and wait for action. Soon Boston & Maine's MB-2 appeared, headed by a brand-new class R-1 number 4114, and so I took this photo. When I got home, I learned of the tragedy of Pearl Harbor. The world was to change forever." Indeed, the war would bring about profound changes for America's railroads and its steam power. *George C. Corey*

PAGE 22: B&M's R-1s were modern Baldwin 4-8-2s with large tenders that offered ample water capacity. It is understood that B&M opted to assign its R-1 Mountain types to the East Wind in order to skip the water stop at Dover, New Hampshire, on the run from Portland, Maine, to Lowell, Massachusetts. Interestingly, Lehigh & Hudson River ordered near copies of this 4-8-2 for fast freight service in 1944. The *East Wind* was a summer-only train connecting Washington, DC, with Maine and operated using distinctively painted canary-yellow passenger cars from 1940 to 1942. While the train was revived after the war, the yellow color was not. *George C. Corey*

PAGE 23: Chesapeake & Ohio's final five 4-8-4s, class J-3a 610 to 614, were built by Lima in 1948, placing them among of the last 4-8-4s built in the United States. On C&O, the 4-8-4 was called Greenbriers instead of using the more common Northern moniker. *G. W. Kowanski*

PAGE 23: Locomotive valve gear serves a function similar to that of a transmission in an automobile. Common valve gear uses a network of rods, eccentrics, and links to allow the engineer to direct the flow of steam to the cylinders. This regulates the power and direction of the engine. Baker valve gear was one of several common arrangements used on late-era steam locomotives such as C&O 614. *Brian Solomon*

PAGE 24: Between 1906 and 1914, Canadian Pacific Railway acquired its first two classes of a 4-6-2 Pacific that were similar in most respects except for the size of the driving wheels. The G1 class, represented by 2201, pictured, featured 75-inch drivers, compared to the more conservative 70-inch wheels on the G2. A total of 39 G1s were built. These were later improved with modern appliances like the Elesco feedwater heater (the laterally mounted cylinder seen atop the smokebox in front of the exhaust stack). By the mid-1950s, CPR had begun to dieselize operations, and a new Montreal Locomotive Works Alco-designed diesel idles alongside the steam locomotives it is intended to replace. *Jim Shaughnessy*

PAGE 25: Canadian National Railways was an early proponent of the 4-8-4 design, and with its American affiliate, Grand Trunk Western, it assembled the largest North American fleet. CNR's 4-8-4s were versatile locomotives; sufficient light axle loading allowed for their operation across the railroad's expansive North American railway network. *Jim Shaughnessy*

PAGE 25: In the 1950s, Jim Shaughnessy traveled far and wide to photograph railroads in action. He made many trips to eastern Canada, where steam survived on a large scale a few years later than on many lines in the United States. A brisk morning on November 11, 1957, at Dorval, Quebec, in suburban Montreal offers an excellent opportunity to capture Canadian National Railways 4-6-2 Pacific 5280 marching eastward with a short passenger train destined for Montreal Central Station. Jim's clever use of cross lighting and low-angle shooting emphasized the morning frost, providing a dramatic portrait of this locomotive at work. At Dorval, both Canadian National and Canadian Pacific double-track lines run parallel, making it a favorite place to catch the action. CPR's tracks can be seen to the right of CNR's lines. *Jim Shaughnessy*

PAGE 25: Canadian National's last order for 4-8-2 Mountain types was for 20 class U-1fs built by Montreal Locomotive Works in 1944. These impressive semistreamlined engines were the railroad's last new steam power and unusually late examples of the 4-8-2 type. CNR 6060 was retired from revenue service in 1959 but restored by the railroad for excursion service a decade later. Subsequent restorations in the 1980s and 1990s have allowed for the engine's continued availability for excursion work; as of 2015, it was based in Alberta. *George W. Kowanski*

PAGE 26: Union Pacific has kept the tradition of steam alive. In the decades since the end of regular steam operation, its final 4-8-4 Northern (variously numbered 844 and 8444) has worked excursions and freights, long after all the railroad's other steam power had been idled by internal-combustion power. In 1981, UP returned 4-6-6-4 Challenger 3985 to service, and as of 2015, UP was aiming to restore Big Boy 4014 to active service as well. *Brian Solomon*

PAGE 27: Delaware, Lackawanna & Western connected the New York City area with Buffalo via Scranton, Pennsylvania. It was no ordinary railroad. In the early twentieth century, it improved its route using exceptionally modern construction aimed at minimizing curvature and maximum gradients. It bought some of Alco's three-cylinder Mountain types beginning in 1925, with five locomotives with 73-inch drivers designed for heavy passenger service. In 1926 and 1927, it followed up with 35 freight-service 4-8-2s with 63-inch drivers that were variously assigned to fast freight and coal services. These were delivered in two batches, with the final 10 featuring nominally more conservative output.

Lackawanna's three-cylinder Mountains worked for more than two decades as built and have been considered some of the best examples of Alco's three-cylinder design. Experiencing a three-cylinder locomotive was a special thrill for the locomotive enthusiast since the machines had a distinctive off-beat exhaust that developed a syncopated sound as it gained speed. Just imagine the sound of this freight as it worked east at Blairstown in western New Jersey on the railroad's famed Lackawanna Cut-Off, a superbly built line that opened in 1908. *Donald W. Furler*

PAGE 29: A few eastern railroads embraced the 4-6-6-4 Challenger type that had been developed by Union Pacific. Unlike ponderous Mallet articulated types that were designed for efficient movement of slow-speed drag freights, the Challenger was an articulated intended for speed and power and well suited to fast freight service. From 1940 to 1941, Western Maryland bought a dozen Baldwin Challengers with enormous boilers to maintain 50 mph in road freight service in level territory while being able to march heavy trains up its ascent of the Alleghenies west of Cumberland, where the ruling grade was 1.75 percent. These were among the heaviest locomotives operated by a Northeastern railroad, tipping the scales at just over 300 tons. *Donald W. Furler*

PAGE 30: Canadian Pacific was an unusual railroad, in that its acquisition of 4-6-2 Pacific types spanned more than four decades and continued despite its investment in larger and more modern types. Steamtown National Historic Site in Scranton, Pennsylvania, is a living museum situated in the heart of an urban industrial environment developed by the old Delaware, Lackawanna & Western Railroad. Steamtown offers a rare glimpse of a steam-era shop complex, while steam excursions over former Lackawanna's mainlines have recreated the spirit of passenger travel in the steam era. *George W. Kowanski*

PAGE 31: Delaware & Hudson faced a difficult climb north from Scranton over Ararat Summit in northeastern Pennsylvania. Among the limitations of steam-era operation was the inability of reciprocating steam locomotives to place maximum power on the rail when starting. To overcome this, helper locomotives were used to move heavy trains in graded territory. In this pair of photos, four locomotives are used to move freight WM-3 with 101 cars, a 4-6-6-4 Challenger in the lead, while at the back another Challenger, combined with a borrowed New York, Ontario & Western Electro-Motive–built FT/FB diesel-set and a D&H 2-8-0 work as helpers. The steam-to-diesel transition occurred over more than two decades, yet photos with both types of power working together are relatively few, and images such as this one of NYO&W diesels working with D&H steam are rare. *Donald W. Furler*

PAGE 32: Erie's Delaware Division (Port Jervis, New York, to Susquehanna, Pennsylvania) was a supremely scenic eastern mainline and a favorite route for photographers. Among the scenic highlights of the route were the double-track bridge across the Delaware River and miles of riverside running. The route is undoubtedly best known for the immense Starrucca Viaduct in northeastern Pennsylvania. This empty coal train will have diverged from the mainline at Lackawaxen to follow Erie's Wyoming Division via Honesdale, returning to coalfields near Scranton. During the World War I period, Erie bought three classes of 2-10-2s for heavy freight work, dividing its orders between all three major builders. The class R-2, as pictured, was one of 30 of the type built by Alco at Schenectady, New York. Erie's final 25 2-10-2s embraced a standard USRA design and were constructed at Alco's Brooks works in Dunkirk, New York, a shop with close historic ties to the Erie. *Donald W. Furler*

PAGE 33: Today, Reading 2100 is stored in Washington State; 2101, which worked the American Freedom Train in the mid-1970s, is now a static display at the Baltimore & Ohio Railroad Museum in Baltimore; 2102 is stored on the Reading & Northern at Port Clinton, Pennsylvania, and may operate again on old home rails; and 2124 is a static exhibit at the Steamtown National Historic Site in Scranton. Sadly, having survived the end of the steam era, Reading 2123 was scrapped in 1964. *Brian Solomon & Richard J. Solomon*

PAGE 34: Union Pacific's 4-12-2s were extraordinarily powerful machines; its main cylinder tractive effort was 96,650 pounds (distinguished from locomotives that derived a portion of slow-speed output from booster engines), the greatest for any nonarticulated steam locomotive. This image provides a good frontal view of the Gresley conjugated valve gear arrangement used to actuate the valve on the central cylinder. UP ordered 88 4-12-2 three-cylinder locomotives from Alco, the most numerous of any Alco three-cylinder design. The center cylinder powered a cranked axle and gave the locomotive six cylinder exhausts per cylinder cycle, which provided more even exhaust and smoother power than two-cylinder types. *Robert A. Witbeck*

PAGE 35: Mexican railroad practices emulated those in the United States but tended to lag behind developments by a few years. This 4-8-4 leading a freight of 40- and 50-foot American boxcars resembles a scene common to many railroads north of the border a decade earlier. By 1961, NdeM was still operating big steam while the large railroads in the United States and Canada were fully dieselized. Mexico bought new steam until 1946. Its dieselization wasn't completed until the mid-1960s. The difference of a few years allowed photographers to record the change, traveling south after steam had finished in America. Notice the brakeman riding atop the second boxcar, a once-standard practice across the continent that was ultimately banned for safety reasons. *Jim Shaughnessy*

PAGE 38: This popular locomotive, known colloquially as "the four and a quarter," has enjoyed an unusually long career. It was one of two 4-6-2s built by the Baldwin Locomotive Works in January 1928 for Gulf, Mobile & Northern (a component company of the Gulf, Mobile & Ohio). It had various owners after G&MO dieselized. Since the mid-1980s, it has been owned by Blue Mountain & Reading/Reading & Northern, where it has been operated as an excursion locomotive. Its blue livery is unusual and is a tribute to some of Reading Company's passenger steam engines that historically wore blue. *Patrick Yough*

PAGES 39, 51, and 52: Erie Railroad bought its first Pacifics in 1905, and over the next 21 years assembled a significant fleet of this type for passenger service. Where its early Pacifics (class K1) had boilers 74.5 inches in diameter, its last Pacifics (class K5, subclasses K5, K5a, and K5b) were wide-boiler machines based on the United States Railroad Administration's "heavy" Pacific plan, with boilers 78 inches in diameter. These were handsome, well-proportioned machines. In their late-era configuration, these engines featured a laterally mounted Elesco feedwater heater ahead of the exhaust stack, which gave them a serious, all-business appearance. While Erie wasn't a major long-distance passenger carrier on par with New York Central System or Pennsylvania Railroad, it operated several fine trains over the length of its Jersey City–Chicago mainline, with several trains offering connections to Buffalo. *Donald W. Furler*

PAGE 40: When it comes to describing steam power, "big" is a relative term. In 1949, few railroaders in the 1940s would have considered this conservatively proportioned Bessemer & Lake Erie 4-6-2 to be a big locomotive. It was certainly wasn't compared with some of the truly massive machines that were working the rails at that time. Yet this Pacific, like so many thousands of locomotives built in the early years of the twentieth century, was part of the big steam trend that characterized locomotive production of the period. Author Angus Sinclair, writing before World War I, would have considered this engine to be *too* big. It was one of only four Pacifics on Bessemer's roster, built by Alco at Schenectady, New York, in 1913 and retired 40 years later. *J. William Vigrass*

PAGE 41: Double heading was the operation of two locomotives together on the front, or head, of the train. This was necessary when one locomotive couldn't supply sufficient power to move a train or meet its schedule, or if a locomotive broke down or a second locomotive needed to be moved. Most railroads avoided the practice whenever possible because it was expensive. Every locomotive required an engineer and a fireman, and wages were a major cost in train operations. For the photographer, a double-headed train was a great thrill; it meant more steam, smoke, and action. *Jim Shaughnessy*

PAGE 43: Baltimore & Ohio train 11, the *Metropolitan Special*, works upgrade at Swanton, Maryland, behind 2-8-2 Mikado 4414 and 4-6-2 Pacific 5086. B&O's old West End ran from Cumberland, Maryland, to Grafton, West Virginia. This route was the stuff of legends. Heading west, the famed 17-Mile Grade was long and steep. However the really difficult pull was eastbound on the Cranberry Grade, which was one of the steepest mainline grades east of the Rockies. This train will crest the 17-Mile Grade at Altamont, Maryland. *Donald W. Furler*

PAGE 44: In their early years, the Pacific type represented the latest in passenger steam power. This rare action photo dates to about 1912. The leaning of the front of the engine is a distortion caused by the camera's vertical focal plane shutter when capturing a rapidly moving subject. *F. H. Worcester, collection of Robert A. Buck*

PAGE 45: New York Central Class K-11c 4-6-2 4461 was a pre–World War I Pacific that had been shifted from premier assignments decades earlier. New York Central routinely reassigned locomotives to lesser duties as new and more powerful locomotives took over. By 1952, diesels were rapidly grabbing all the premier trains, and even New York Central's famed J-class Hudsons had been reduced to working freight. *Donald W. Furler*

PAGE 47: Pennsylvania Railroad's class K4s was the most famous of all the 4-6-2 Pacific types. PRR's designation was confusing: When it began introducing superheating, it added a small s at the end of the locomotive designation to indicate that the locomotive type was superheated. In these situations, the s doesn't infer plural. Some authors have tried to avoid confusion by truncating the classification to K4, but this is technically incorrect. Furthermore, in later years, when all its new steam power was superheated, PRR stopped assigning the s to new classes of locomotive. Thus there are no M1s, J1s, or T1s locomotives although all were superheated. *Robert A. Witbeck*

PAGE 48: In the steam era, Pennsylvania Railroad was America's largest railroad. Known as Pennsy to its fans, it operated the most passenger trains and carried the largest volume of passengers. Its K4s Pacific was its most common twentieth century passenger locomotive. Among its last regular assignments was working New Jersey suburban services on the New York & Long Branch to Bay Head Junction. *Donald W. Furler*

PAGE 49: Every photograph has a story. George C. Corey made this image in December 1945, and explains, "By now the B&M had received two E7s (Electro-Motive passenger diesels), so while the P-4s were still working some of the premier trains, trouble was on the horizon. This photo shows the postwar appearance of these engines following the removal of smoke deflectors and the installation of duel front-mounted air pumps behind shields. While better looking in this postwar configuration, I still preferred them in their glory days." *George C. Corey*

PAGE 50: By 1949, Boston & Maine had received enough diesels to handle the premier runs, and its P-4 Pacifics had been relegated to working secondary trains such as this empty milk run—their glory days were over. Within a few years, big steam would be gone from the B&M. While engine 3712 was scrapped, its sister 3713 survives. It's part of the Steamtown collection at Scranton, Pennsylvania, and a candidate for operational restoration. *George C. Corey*

PAGE 53: Boston & Albany's 20 class J-2 Hudsons were patterned on New York Central's successful J-1 design but featured slightly smaller drive wheels (75 inches compared with 79 inches on the J-1) to better suit the traction requirements imposed by B&A's steep grades. The first 10 J-2s (subclasses J-2 and J-2a) were built by Alco, the second 10 by Lima (subclass J-2b). While finding a J-2 working a B&A passenger train in 1945 was a common and expected occurrence, photographer Bob Buck was still delighted to take this photo of this locomotive at Palmer's Union Station. Today, if a Hudson arrived in Palmer, it would attract hundreds, if not thousands, of people. Sadly all of B&A's Hudsons, as well all of Central's, were sent to scrap, denying future generations the ability to witness one of the finest passenger locomotives ever built. *Robert A. Buck*

PAGE 54: New York Central's J-3a Hudsons have been described as thoroughbreds—racehorses made from highly refined machinery. The most famous were the streamlined engines using Henry Dreyfuss's classic treatment, which was initially applied to 10 brand new J-3a's in 1938. For 15-year old John Pickett, who took this photo on March 16, 1946, at Palentine Bridge, New York, they were a thrill to see at speed. By this point, this engine had endured almost eight years of hard service, much of it during the punishing years of World War II traffic, and it's showing signs of heavy use. *John E. Pickett*

PAGE 55: Lima built 10 J-2c class 4-6-4s for Boston & Albany in 1931, making them something of an orphan type on the New York Central System. All the other 4-6-4s on New York Central's lines were designed and built by Alco at its Schenectady, New York, plant. By the time of this photo, taken in June 1949, steam operations were nearing their end on B&A, most of the A1 class Berkshires were out of service on freight, and diesels were working many trains. The end came less than two years later when a New York Central Mohawk made a well-publicized final run over the line. *Robert A. Buck*

PAGE 56: Despite being one of the most perfectly executed steam locomotive designs of all time, New York Central's Hudson type couldn't match the economies of diesel power. While it was the pride of the railroad's fleet, in the 1950s, railroad management lacked nostalgic sympathies, and this historically significant type was lost forever. *John E. Picket*

PAGE 58: Nickel Plate's first four 4-6-4s, class L-1a, were built by Alco in 1927 and delivered shortly after New York Central's famous pioneers. Its four later locomotives, class L-1b numbered 174–177, were built by Lima in 1929. Nickel Plate's Hudson types were among the smallest built and some of the few that regularly worked in freight service. On most railroads, Hudsons were exclusively passenger engines, owing to the operating characteristics associated with their design. Nickel Plate's first Hudson, engine 170, was preserved after its retirement in 1957 and is now a static display at the St. Louis Museum of Transportation in Kirkwood, Missouri. *J. William Vigrass*

PAGE 59: In 1935, Milwaukee Road challenged the running times offered by streamlined articulated diesel trains with its shrouded, modern, lightweight Atlantics. These locomotives were so successful in attracting passengers that Milwaukee returned to Alco for more powerful streamlined steam power. In August 1938, Alco delivered six elegant, streamlined 4-6-4 Hudsons to Milwaukee Road. These were classified as its F7s and used a streamlining treatment similar to the A-class Atlantics but were designed by industrial designer Otto Kuhler, who applied a distinctive "futuristic" styling. *John E. Pickett collection*

PAGE 61: After almost six decades of static display, Santa Fe 3463 may again roll under its own power. The Coalition for Sustainable Rail has the noble goal of restoring Santa Fe 3463 to service as a test bed for advanced steam locomotive design and hopes to ultimately produce a modern, thermodynamically efficient, and low-maintenance steam locomotive. *John E. Pickett collection*

PAGE 63: Most famous of all 4-6-4s were Canadian Pacific's Royal Hudsons, named in honor of the two engines that hauled special trains carrying King George VI and Queen Elizabeth during their visit to Canada in 1939. *George W. Kowanski*

PAGE 66: Chicago, Burlington & Quincy received eight 4-8-4s from Baldwin in 1930 and opted to build 28 similar machines at its West Burlington, Iowa, shops between 1936 and 1940. The Baldwins were classed as O-5, and the homebuilds were O-5A. Interestingly, CB&Q had also assigned Class O designations to its fleet of 2-8-2 Mikados, but for every 4-8-4, CB&Q had nearly 10 Mikados. *Jim Shaughnessy*

PAGE 67: Milwaukee Road's prewar S-2 class 4-8-4s were built to a different design than its World War II–era S-3 Class. Its 40 S-2s were built by Baldwin, while its 10 S-3s were built by Alco using a copy of a Delaware & Hudson design with a few Milwaukee Road trappings, such as the vestibule-styled cab. Two of the S-3s have been preserved. Locomotive 261 is a popular excursion engine maintained and operated by North Star Rail and based in Minneapolis, Minnesota, while 265 is a static display at the Illinois Railway Museum at Union, Illinois. *John E. Pickett*

PAGE 70: On many railroads, Mikados were the most common workhorse, but they were too often ignored by photographers, who tended to focus on the more glamorous passenger engines or the larger freight engines. Toward the end of World War I, USRA allocated some light Mikados for Central Railroad of New Jersey, and after the war it continued to buy engines of roughly the same pattern. These were solid, well-built machines that hauled the company's tonnage for more than two decades until diesels took over after World War II. *Donald W. Furler*

PAGES 68–69: Grand Trunk Western used 4-8-4 designs for nearly the same purposes as its parent, Canadian National Railways. However, while CNR's locomotives were built in Canada, GTW's engines were constructed in the United States. GTW 6325 is a class U3b built by American Locomotive Company at Schenectady, New York, in February 1942. After retirement in 1959, it was displayed for more than a quarter century at Battle Creek, Michigan. Later it was acquired by Ohio Central and returned to operating condition, where it served as a popular excursion locomotive. *Chris Bost*

PAGES 71, 76, and 77: Photographer John Gruber writes, "An extraordinary, unexpected experience—nine days with Southern 4501 on a 1,450-mile shakedown trip from Chattanooga to Louisville, Asheville, Salisbury, and Richmond in August 1966. We were guests of W. Graham and Frances Claytor in a Southern business car, traveling in style. Graham, then vice president, went on to become president of Southern and president of Amtrak. The trip was a day longer than expected because of a broken spring hanger on the locomotive (delaying the Sparkplug, a fast auto parts freight train), which was repaired the next morning. There was apprehension, meeting Southern president D. W. Brosnan on the platform at Asheville (all went well). For the whole time, I had full access to the locomotive and its crew. David P. Morgan, *Trains* editor, wrote a book about the trip, *Locomotive 4501* (1968); I was the principal photographer. It was good to see the 4501 back in service in fall 2014, painted black as a freight locomotive should be painted. But I missed the green and gold (Southern's passenger colors) from its first return to excursion service in 1966." *John Gruber*

PAGE 73: Illinois Central was unusual in that it continued to build many of its own locomotives years after the majority of American lines relied entirely on commercial builders. Locomotive 2524 was one of 55 4-8-2 Mountain types constructed at IC's Paducah, Kentucky, shops using the boilers from outdated 2-10-2s. Later, IC built a group of 2600 series 4-8-2s from scratch. IC's loyalty to coal contributed to its continued operation of mainline steam as late as 1960. This spectacular February view was made shortly before the end of regular steam operations. *Ron Wright*

PAGE 75: In 1923, Pennsylvania Railroad built its first 4-8-2, classed M1, a new type that was derived from the railroad's successful I1s Decapod and that used many similar parts. After two years of testing, PRR ordered 200 of them, then in 1930, it ordered another 100 locomotives of a similar design, class M1a. All big-boiler Mountains were highly regarded by PRR steam men; these were capable locomotives that worked fast freights until the 1950s. *Ron Wright*

PAGE 79: Photographer George C. Corey explains, "In 1947, Baltimore & Ohio bought 13 of the 18 B&M Mountain types that had been rendered surplus by diesels. Apparently the B&O liked these engines as they were among the last B&O steam to run in 1958. On July 30, 1956, I photographed B&O 5651 double-headed with a Q-4 Mikado pulling out of a siding at Attica Junction, Ohio. Stan K. Bolton and I had chased this train out of Willard. We were told that this was the Banana Train, headed for Toledo with 18 cars of bananas and 100 cars of coal. At Attica Junction, it took the siding to let a Time-Saver Freight go by, and it followed that job to Toledo Junction, but I don't think the crew saw any yellow signals; [the Time-Saver] went by us with three EMD F-7s at about 70 [mph]. Not that a B&M 4100 . . . excuse me a B&O 5650 . . . couldn't have made that speed." *George C. Corey*

PAGE 81: In 1927, Lackawanna was the first eastern railroad in the United States to buy 4-8-4s. It called them Poconos rather than Northerns and eventually rostered 45 of the type. The 1644 was one of the last 10 built, delivered in 1934, and designed for freight and passenger service. While DL&W had electrified its busy suburban passenger services, its long-distance trains were hauled by steam. In 1949, three years after this photo was exposed, DL&W upgraded its flagship passenger train, replacing the heavyweight steam-hauled *Lackawanna Limited* with a diesel streamliner called the *Phoebe Snow*, named after the mythical character created in the early twentieth century to promote Lackawanna's premier passenger train and its primary commodity: anthracite coal. *Donald W. Furler*

PAGE 82: Photographer Robert A. Buck grew up within sight of Boston & Albany's mainline in Warren, Massachusetts. As a youngster barely old enough to stand, he watched from the window of his house as B&A's ponderous 1300-series Mallets worked freight through town. Bob grew up with the Berkshires, Hudsons, Mikados, and Pacifics that were the order of the day in the 1930s and 1940s. As a teenager, he befriended crews and spent his free time photographing his favorite railroad, putting his memories on film for new generations to appreciate. *Robert A. Buck*

PAGE 84: Pennsylvania Railroad hauled freight using a variety of well-built big steam, including an enormous roster of 2-8-0s, 2-8-2s, 2-10-0s, 4-8-2s, and some World War II–era 2-10-4s, among other types. However, it never ordered any 2-8-4s, so this view of Nickel Plate Road 759 makes for an unusual scene at the west portal of the Gallitzin tunnels. *George W. Kowanski*

PAGE 85: Baldwin built Santa Fe's 15 4101-class 2-8-4s in 1927. During World War II, Santa Fe inherited seven former Boston & Maine Lima-built 2-8-4s that were near copies of the original A-1 type but with Coffin feedwater heaters instead of Elescos. In this view, Santa Fe 2-8-4 4114 appears to be relatively new. *John Pickett collection*

PAGE 86: Originally Erie assigned its Berkshires to freight service between Hornell, New York, and Marion, Ohio, but they eventually expanded their territory. In later years, they often worked the east end of the railroad. *Donald W. Furler*

PAGE 87: Delaware, Lackawanna & Western bought two batches of Alco three-cylinder Mountain types. The first five, delivered in 1925, were passenger locomotives, while the second batch of 35 locomotives—delivered during 1926 and 1927—were heavy freight locomotives. In 1940, engine 2228, leading an eastward freight, has just emerged from the Roseville Tunnel east of Andover, New Jersey. *Donald W. Furler*

PAGE 89: Southern Pacific's affiliate, St. Louis Southwestern, was known by its trade name, Cotton Belt. Between 1986 and 1993, former Cotton Belt 819 regularly impressed the public with displays of its power on the lines where decades earlier it earned its keep hauling revenue trains. This was one of 10 4-8-4s constructed by the railroad's Pine Bluff, Arkansas, shops during World War II. Retired at the end of Cotton Belt's steam operations, it was preserved and then resurrected and restored in 1986 to service at the Pine Bluff shops by the Cotton Belt Rail Historical Society and the Arkansas Railroad Club. Old 819 operated in excursion service until 1993. As an excursion engine, it wasn't as well known as other heavy-duty modern steam locomotives. But it put on quite a show and kept dispatchers happy by being able to run ahead of high-priority freights, maintaining its legacy as a high-performance machine. As of 2015, the locomotive was being overhauled. *Tom Kline*

PAGE 92: Santa Fe's later Northerns, those built by Baldwin between 1938 and 1944, have been considered among the best of the type. These came in three orders, each identified by an individual class as distinguished by the first locomotive in each group. Engine 3783 was one of the 3776-class locomotives built in 1941, and like other top-class Northerns, featured 80-inch drivers and 28x32-inch cylinders and operated at 300 psi boiler pressure. The 2900s were similar but were built during World War II and as a result were constructed using heavier materials, leading to a slightly greater engine weight. *Robert A. Witbeck*

PAGE 93: Southern Pacific's original streamlined 4-8-4s, class GS2, were built with tenders shaped to conform to the width and profile of the streamlined passenger cars they were designed to haul, thus maintaining visual integrity throughout the length of the new train. These tenders were carried by six-wheel trucks to better distribute its weight and had capacity for 22,000 gallons of water and 6,275 gallons of fuel oil. This view is of the tender for SP GS4 4447, sister engine to the famous 4449; it was built a few years later than tenders for the GS2s, yet featured similar proportions, although it had an additional 1,300 gallons of water capacity. Notice the unusual rear-facing light. *Robert A. Witbeck*

PAGE 93: A radio commentator described Southern Pacific's reequipped *Daylight* of 1940 as "the world's most beautiful train," which echoed SP's sentiments. After its retirement from revenue service in the 1950s, Southern Pacific GS-4 4449 was displayed in a Portland, Oregon, park. In the mid-1970s, it was restored in a red, white, and blue livery to haul the American Freedom Train as part of the nation's bicentennial celebrations. In the early 1980s, it was restored in its original red, orange, black, and silver for operation to the 1981 Sacramento Railfair. Since that time, 4449 has made regular appearances as a mainline excursion locomotive and remains one of America's most popular locomotives. *George W. Kowanski*

PAGE 93: The undeniable glamour associated with SP's *Daylight* passenger trains has continued to fascinate new generations with big steam and allowed repeated restorations for some of America's finest locomotives. Who could have imagined back in 1941, when SP GS-4 4449 was new, that more than 70 years later the locomotive would still be serviceable and enjoying an enormous public following.

SP GS-4 4449 was retired in 1957 and put on display in Portland, Oregon. In 1974, it was restored to operating condition for service on the American Freedom Train, a specially appointed train created to commemorate America's bicentennial. After a brief period in storage, the locomotive was returned to steam excursion service in 1981, this time wearing its original *Daylight* livery. Later, it briefly reverted to the 1970s red, white, and blue dress. The locomotive was overhauled in 2013; it resides at the Oregon Rail Heritage Center when not working excursions. *Tom Kline*

PAGE 94: US Highway 30 runs parallel to Union Pacific's transcontinental mainline across central Nebraska, making it a popular route for railroad photographers in the days of steam. Once in sight, this highway allowed a photographer to pursue his quarry for miles across the cornfields. *Jim Shaughnessy*

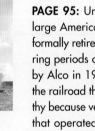

PAGE 95: Union Pacific's 844 is unique among large American locomotives because it was never formally retired and has remained serviceable (barring periods of necessary repair) since it was built by Alco in 1944; furthermore, it is still owned by the railroad that bought it. This last fact is noteworthy because very few American railroad companies that operated steam have survived the waves of mergers and consolidation that have swept through the industry since the late 1950s. Union Pacific had renumbered its 4-8-4 844 as 8444 to make room for a GP30 diesel that required that road number. After the GP30 was retired, the 4-8-4 reclaimed its historic road number. *George W. Kowanski*

PAGE 96: Reading & Northern began in 1983 as Conrail-spinoff Blue Mountain & Reading, operating on a short section of former Pennsylvania Railroad trackage running north from Reading, Pennsylvania. Over the next three decades, it expanded through acquisition of former Conrail lines in eastern Pennsylvania to form a network of former Reading Company, Lehigh Valley, and CNJ lines in anthracite coal-mining country. In addition to diesels for freight service, it has operated two preserved steam locomotives: former Gulf, Mobile & Northern Baldwin-built 4-6-2 Pacific No.425 and former Reading Company class T-1 4-8-4 Northern No. 2102, both pictured in a staged night photo shoot at the old Reading Company shops on June 28, 1986. *Chris Bost*

PAGE 98: Contrasts in technology: Reading's T-1 2127 was a late-era steam design; at the time of this photo in the late 1940s, it was a nearly new machine while the signals to the left are true antiques. The lower two signalheads are Hall disc signals, a type of hardware patented in the 1870s as one of the first commercially available automatic block signals. Although obsolete by 1900, Reading Company continued to install them as late as World War I. *John Pickett collection*

PAGE 104: An eastbound Western Maryland coal train is seen crossing the Keystone Viaduct, east of Meyersdale, Pennsylvania, where WM's single-track mainline crossed over Baltimore & Ohio's parallel double-track line. Engine 1117 was one of the railroad's 2-10-0 Decapods, which at 420,000 pounds were the largest engines of this wheel arrangement ever built, even heavier than PRR's I1s. The railroad at this location was abandoned, and the old roadbed is part of the Great Allegheny Passage trail. *Donald W. Furler*

PAGE 105: Pennsylvania Railroad's Elmira Branch was a route used to forward coal from central Pennsylvania mines northward to the Lake Ontario port at Sodus Point, where much of the traffic was destined for Canadian markets via lake boats. In the late 1920s, the port had expanded its pier, allowing it to fill two lake boats simultaneously. Facilities were further expanded during World War II and again in 1952. Coal traffic via Elmira Branch experienced rapid growth during the 1950s; at its peak, there were as many as six heavily loaded trains traveling the line every day. For steam enthusiasts, it was one of the last places where PRR regularly worked big steam with its I1s "Hippos" for freight traffic until 1957. *Ron Wright*

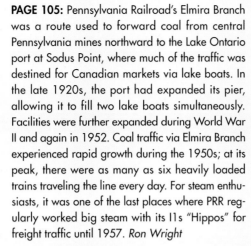

PAGE 107: By 1957, photographers looking to capture the end of steam were rapidly running out of time. Pennsylvania's rural Elmira Branch ran north from Williamstown, Pennsylvania, via Elmira, New York, to Sodus Point and hosted heavy steam later than many lines in the region. Some photographers avoided the line because the heaviest trains were all northbound, and the feeling was that since the action was coming "out of the sun," the operations were unfavorable for classic action photographs. This didn't deter Jim Shaughnessy, who made several productive trips along the Elmira Branch and exposed dozens of iconic scenes, including those reproduced here. *Jim Shaughnessy*

PAGE 108: This Santa Fe Santa Fe-type (which appears redundant, but isn't), having worked as a helper on the steep grades over Cajon Pass, waits to return downgrade. While the 2-10-2s were largely known as Santa Fe types, Southern Pacific found it unpalatable to refer to locomotives by its competitor's name and called its 2-10-2s Decks (short for Decapod, the term usually reserved for 2-10-0s). *John E. Pickett*

PAGE 109: Baltimore & Ohio's line from Cumberland, Maryland, to Connellsville, Pennsylvania, crossed the famed Sand Patch grade in southwestern Pennsylvania. This was B&O's mainline to Chicago and served as a primary trunk for through traffic. The grade takes its unusual name from the place-name at the summit, where the line crests in a long tunnel. Sand Patch has always been a place for heavy action. B&O was one of the first railroads to take advantage of the 2-10-2 as a heavy road locomotive. Its first of the type were built in 1914. The locomotives pictured here were of the powerful S-1 class built in the early 1920s. *Donald W. Furler*

PAGE 110: Pennsylvania Railroad's 125 2-10-4s represented an anomaly for its steam designs. While PRR had a long tradition of designing its own steam power and favored the Belpaire Boiler with its wide, boxy firebox, the World War II–era J-class 2-10-4s used an established design borrowed from Chesapeake & Ohio. If PRR had had its druthers, it would have built freight Duplex types based on its own research. Interestingly, the J class and postwar Q2 Duplexes were similarly proportioned—the Q2 used a 4-4-6-4 wheel arrangement that essentially divided 10 drive wheels between two sets of cylinders in an effort to lower the piston thrust and reduce the weight of reciprocating parts. *Robert A. Witbeck*

PAGE 112: Alco-Schenectady built 10 2-10-4 Texas types for Central Vermont Railway in 1928. At the time, CV had only recently become part of the Canadian National system. The north end of the railroad had been damaged by Vermont's great flood of November 1927, and rebuilding the railroad to modern standards after the flood allowed for operation of much larger motive power. *George C. Corey*

PAGE 115: Southern Pacific was first and foremost in the adoption of the 4-10-2, a three-cylinder single-expansion engine known as the Southern Pacific type. The only other railroad to use them was Union Pacific, which bought 10. Although unusual, SP got good service from its three-cylinder engines, many of which worked for more than two decades in hard service. Garnet is a remote desert location on SP's Sunset Route on the east slope of the climb over Beaumont Pass. *Robert A. Witbeck*

PAGE 117: Virginian was a high-volume bituminous conduit built in the early twentieth century to high modern standards. The mainline was completed in 1909 and ran 443 miles from Deepwater, West Virginia, to a Hampton Roads coal port at Sewells Point, Virginia. Virginian's late-era construction permitted operation of some of the largest steam locomotives ever built. It took an experimental Baldwin triplex in 1916, which proved to be a failure in service. Then, in 1918, it acquired 10 Alco-built 2-10-10-2s, which were remarkably successful and had long service lives. Virginian's 2-10-10-2s had tremendous pulling power and were rated to deliver 176,600 pounds tractive effort—the highest rating given to any reciprocating steam locomotive. *John E. Pickett collection*

PAGE 118: Bearing a resemblance to Baltimore & Ohio's pioneer Mallet, "Old Maude," is this nameless Western Maryland 0-6-6-0. Although into its fourth decade of service at the time of this photo in summer 1950, it isn't quite as old as it looks. It was one of nine Baldwin 2-6-6-2s built between 1909 and 1910 but later converted to 0-6-6-0s for yard service. Very few Mallets survived into the diesel era with their original compound arrangement. Notice the large low-pressure cylinders with D-slide valves on the forward engine, which immediately identify this locomotive as a compound, as distinguished from later single-expansion articulated types. By the end of 1951, this old machine was finally off the roster. *George C. Corey*

PAGE 119: Milwaukee Road 92 was built by Alco's Schenectady Locomotive Works in 1912 as a 2-6-6-2 Mallet compound for freight work on the railroad's Pacific Extension. Later it was rebuilt as a single-expansion engine. Milwaukee's Pacific Extension was most famous as a pioneer application for General Electric's direct-current mainline electrification. *John E. Pickett collection*

PAGE 120: Norfolk & Western's Y6b was its final type of road freight steam built for road freight service. The class was an advancement on its earlier 2-8-8-2 Mallets. The company's Roanoke Shops built three groups of Y6bs between 1948 and 1952. Locomotive 2177, seen here working as a pusher, was one of the first seven locomotives. The last of the group only worked for eight years before steam ended in 1960. *Ron Wright*

PAGE 121: On July 26, 1955, John Pickett had a rare opportunity to experience a Southern Pacific cab-forward up close: "I was traveling with two friends. We were going from Klamath Falls [Oregon] to Wendel [California] and Sparks [Nevada]. Driving south we came across this freight, train 553, near Madeline. It was in the hole [on the siding] waiting for another train to come the other way. The crew was cordial and offered us a cab ride. Two of us rode the engine, while one of my friends drove my car. The thing that struck me was that in the cab the locomotive didn't make a 'chuff chuff' sound but more of a whooshing noise, which wasn't what I expected. When we got to Wendel, they changed crews and we had dinner with the guys we rode down with. We spent the night there and in the darkness one of SP's 'back cab' Lima-built AC9s came in. I saw it. But by morning it was gone so I never got a photo." *John E. Pickett collection*

PAGES 123–124: After revenue steam finished in the United States, photographers seeking to document their favorite engines in action looked south of the border, where American-built steam continued to operate into the 1960s. Mexican locomotive and railroad practices were similar to those in the United States, and most Mexican locomotives were supplied by American builders. National Railways of Mexico (Ferrocarriles Nacionales de Mexico) operated some late-era 2-6-6-2s that were rare examples of that type built as single-expansion engines rather than Mallet compounds. *Credit individual photos to John E. Pickett collection and Jim Shaughnessy, respectively*

PAGES 126–127: In the mid-1930s, N&W developed its A-class 2-6-6-4s for fast freight. Unlike its Y-class articulateds, which were advanced Mallet types, its A-class engines were modern single-expansion locomotives (all cylinders received high-pressure steam directly from the boiler) and featured tall drivers with a high-capacity boiler. A total of 43 were built, giving N&W by far the largest number of the relatively unusual 2-6-6-4 arrangement. The last group were completed between 1949 and 1950. *Credit individual photos to Richard J. Solomon and George W. Kowanski, respectively*

PAGE 128: Denver, Rio Grande & Western's crossing of Colorado's Front Range via the Moffat Tunnel route mandated the use of helpers on heavy freights. By the mid-1950s, diesels tended to work the head of through "drag" freights (low-priority, heavy-tonnage trains), but steam locomotives were still being used as pushers on steeply graded portions of the line. The big 2-8-8-2 was added to the back of this eastward train at Tabernash. In the final view (on page 129), it is seen shoving just east of the east switch of Fraser siding. This view is looking geographic-south toward the Gore Range. At this point, the grade has just steepened to 2 percent (compensated for curvature), and the freight requires a steady push to keep moving. *Robert A. Witbeck*

PAGE 130: John Pickett said, "The morning light at Livingston, Montana, was superb for photography" as he recalled September 18, 1952, the day this photo was exposed. By that time, Northern Pacific had reassigned its largest steam power, the famous 2-8-8-4 Yellowstones, to work as helpers on Bozeman Pass. This was a step down from their heyday, when they led freights east from Glendive, Montana, on their namesake division. *John E. Pickett*

PAGE 131: Baldwin built all of SP's cab-forward, single-expansion articulateds. Although the original cab-forward Mallets were specifically designed to combat operating difficulties faced on California's Sierra crossing over Donner Pass, SP used cab-forwards across its Pacific lines. This view appears to be of a freight paused on its descent of Donner's east slope, probably in Cold Stream Canyon west of Truckee. The last SP cab-forward class AC-12 (engine 4294, built in 1944) was preserved after its retirement; today it is a prominent display at the California State Railroad Museum in Sacramento. It is the only survivor of this style of engine. *Robert A. Witbeck*

PAGES 132–133: Duluth, Missabe & Iron Range was among the last railroads in the United States to operate big steam in revenue mainline service. On July 5, 1960, engine 222, one of its massive Baldwin Yellowstones, made a round-trip from Duluth. The company photographer was documenting the occasion, and the northward train with empties carried a caboose at the head end with recording equipment. Three young enthusiasts were also on hand to photograph and document the event. Ron Wright was traveling with his friends Victor Hand and Don Phillips. "We rented a cab for the day, and the taxi driver really got into it. He had a really good time and I think we got better pictures than the company photographer." There would be no second chance. On the return run, 222 had about 10,000 tons of ore in tow. *Ron Wright*

PAGE 134: Southern Pacific's class AC-9s were rare birds. These 12 modern 2-8-8-4 articulateds were SP's only single-expansion locomotives bought new in the conventional orientation and purchased for fast freight service on the Rio Grande Division. All the others were SP's peculiar cab-forward types. *Robert A. Witbeck*

PAGE 135: In this 1982 view, Union Pacific's 3985 was a coal-fired locomotive, and coal is evident in the pile seen atop the tender. During its second life as an excursion engine, UP later converted 3985 to work as an oil burner. In oil-burning configuration, the engine's semi-permanently coupled 14-wheel tender was arranged to carry 25,000 gallons of water and 6,450 gallons of fuel oil. *George W. Kowanski*

PAGES 136–137: Northern Pacific operated three classes of Challengers on its western lines. The pair pictured were two of the 21 class Z-6 built by Alco during 1936 and 1937. Although these locomotives worked for the better part of two decades, photographs of them in action are relatively rare. *John E. Pickett*

PAGE 140: On April 20, 1952, northward Delaware & Hudson symbol freight WR-3 had 108 cars. Leading was Challenger 1538, while at the back were Challengers 1523 and 1525, plus 2-8-0 1207. Each locomotive had its own crew. At the time of this photograph, the end was near for big steam on the D&H; the railroad was fully dieselized by July 1953. It replaced its relatively modern steam with a utilitarian fleet of Alco-GE RS-2 and RS-3 1,500 horsepower road switchers. *Donald W. Furler*

PAGE 141: July 11, 1951, was a good day for action on Western Maryland. Western Maryland's high-priority fast-freight symbol WM-1 warranted lots of power to get it up the grade west of Cumberland. Challenger 1208 is in the lead, and the smoke in the background comes from sister engine 1201 working as midtrain helper. At the back of the train, pushing behind the caboose is engine 1121, one of the railroad's huge Decapods. Back then this was a routine occurrence; today this section of the line is operated with steam by the Western Maryland Scenic Railway, and when they run steam on freight, they sell tickets for the experience. *George C. Corey*

PAGE 141: On this day, Western Maryland Challenger 1204 worked the head end of WM-3, with Decapod 1119 as midtrain helper and 1203 at the back as a pusher. Despite this grand display of power, in general Western Maryland's Baldwin 4-6-6-4s weren't viewed as successful locomotives; they were reported to have been hard on the track. Originally they were intended to work all the way from Hagerstown, Maryland, to Connellsville, Pennsylvania. However, after WM acquired a dozen modern 4-8-4s in 1947, the Challengers were largely relegated to work west of Cumberland, with the 4-8-4 working the east end of the railroad. Ironically, it seems that WM bought the 4-6-6-4s to replace its Decapods, but as it turned out the Challengers were all out of service by 1953, and Decapods outlasted them by a year or so. *George C. Corey*

TABLE OF CONTENTS and PAGE 142: In 1941, Union Pacific expanded its successful 4-6-6-4 Challenger design into the even larger 4-8-8-4 type; soon known as the Big Boy, it is now world famous despite the relatively few engines built and their remote operating territory. Even more remarkable, of the 25 engines built, eight have been preserved. *Robert A. Witbeck*

PAGE 143: Big Boy's maximum output has been estimated at being close to 7,500 horsepower, far greater than Electro-Motive's commercially built four-unit FT freight diesel. Even today, there are no single-unit diesel-electrics that can equal the output of the 4-8-8-4 steam locomotive. However, where the diesel can apply full power to rail when starting a train, Big Boy's maximum occurred at about 30 mph. How close was this Big Boy to its maximum output when it worked Sherman Hill in July 1955? *Jim Shaughnessy*

PAGE 144: With its four 23.75x32-inch cylinders and a boiler that operated at 300 psi, the Big Boy produced 135,375 pounds of tractive effort—approximately 40 percent more than UP's Challengers. Yet where the Challenger could work most UP mainlines, the Big Boys faced limited service territory as a direct result of their restrictive size. What restricted Big Boy's general operation was its unusual length, which made it too long to fit on turntables and other servicing tracks. Typically Big Boys worked as intended over UP's mainline Cheyenne and Ogden and occasionally south from Cheyenne to Denver. *Jim Shaughnessy*

PAGE 144: Of the 25 Union Pacific Big Boys built, 8 were preserved. Since many classes of American steam entirely vanished under the scrapper's torch, this is an outstanding preservation record. Alfred Bruce estimated that the Big Boys represented just 0.8 percent of the total production of approximately 3,100 articulated locomotives built in the Unites States. Today, Union Pacific 4017 is displayed at the National Museum in Green Bay, Wisconsin, where it stands protected in a climate-controlled environment. *Jim Shaughnessy*

PAGE 145: After more than a half-century's slumber, a Big Boy may steam again. When they worked the rails, relatively few people had the pleasure of seeing the Big Boys on the move. Following engine 4014's high-profile restoration, it will undoubtedly be one of the world's most closely followed locomotives. *John Gruber*

PAGE 147: Virginian's highly engineered line allowed it to operate some of the most extreme steam locomotives ever built. This included its massive class XA 2-8-8-8-4 Triplex of 1916, the even more powerful class AE 2-10-10-2s of 1918, and finally copies of Chesapeake & Ohio's 2-6-6-6 Allegheny, built in 1945. Originally it was believed that these locomotives were heavier than C&O's engines, but post–steam era reporting revealed that the weight on the C&O 2-6-6-6 had been misrepresented, and it turned out that C&O's engines were not only heavier than Virginian's, but were actually the heaviest of all steam reciprocating locomotives, weighing in at 778,000 pounds. *John E. Pickett*

PAGES 148–149: Size is all relative to expectations: the last order for the Yellowstones were fulfilled by Baldwin between 1944 and 1945 for Baltimore & Ohio. Compared to Northern Pacific's original massive Z-5 2-8-8-4s, B&O's EM-1s were lightweights, even though they were the largest locomotives on the Baltimore & Ohio. Sadly all were scrapped at the end of the steam era. The only surviving examples of the Yellowstone type are three Duluth, Missabe & Iron Range locomotives displayed in northern Minnesota. *J. William Vigrass*

Bibliography

Books

1846–1896 Fiftieth Anniversary of the Incorporation of the Pennsylvania Railroad Company. Philadelphia: Pennsylvania Railroad, 1896.

Alexander, Edwin P. *American Locomotives.* New York: Bonanza, 1950.

Alymer-Small, Sidney. *The Art of Railroading, Vol. VIII.* Chicago: Railway Publication Society, 1908.

American Railroad Journal—1966. San Marino, CA: Golden West Books, 1965.

Armstrong, John H. *The Railroad—What It Is, What It Does.* Omaha: Simmons-Boardman Publishing, 1982.

Bruccoli Clark Layman, Inc., and Facts on File, Inc. *Encyclopedia of American Business History and Biography: Railroads in the Nineteenth Century.* Bruccoli Clark Layman, Inc., and Facts on File, Inc., 1988.

Bruce, Alfred W. *The Steam Locomotive in America.* New York: W.W. Norton, 1952.

Burgess, George H., and Miles C. Kennedy. *Centennial History of the Pennsylvania Railroad.* Philadelphia: Pennsylvania Railroad,1949.

Bush, Donald J. *The Streamlined Decade.* New York: George Braziller, 1975.

Churella, Albert J. *From Steam to Diesel.* Princeton, NJ: Princeton University Press, 1998.

Collias, Joe G. *Mopac Power—Missouri Pacific Lines, Locomotives and Trains 1905–1955.* San Diego, CA: Howell-North Books, 1980.

Conrad, J. David. *The Steam Locomotive Directory of North America. Vols. I & II.* Polo, IL: Transportation Trails, 1988.

Diesel Locomotive Roster—the Railroad Magazine Series. New York: Wayner Publications, n.d.

Dixon, Thomas W., Jr. *Chesapeake & Ohio—Superpower to Diesels.* Newton, NJ: Carstens Publications, 1984.

Drury, George H. *Guide to North American Steam Locomotives.* Waukesha, WI: Kalmbach Publications, 1993.

Dubin, Arthur D. *Some Classic Trains.* Milwaukee: Kalmbach Publications, 1964.

———. *More Classic Trains.* Milwaukee: Kalmbach Publications, 1974.

Dunscomb, Guy, L. *A Century of Southern Pacific Steam Locomotives.* Modesto, CA: self-published, 1963.

Farrington, S. Kip., Jr. *Railroading from the Head End.* Garden City, New York: Doubleday, Doran and Co., 1943.

———. *Railroading from the Rear End.* New York, Coward McCann,1946.

———. *Railroading the Modern Way.* New York: Coward McCann, 1951.

———. *Railroads at War.* New York: Coward McCann, 1944.

Forney, M. N. *Catechism of the Locomotive.* New York: The Railroad Gazette, 1876.

Gruber, John, and Brian Solomon. *The Milwaukee Road's Hiawathas.* St. Paul, MN: Voyageur Press, 2006.

Hampton, Taylor. *The Nickel Plate Road.* Cleveland, OH: The World Publishing Co., 1947.

Harding, J. W. and Frank Williams. *Locomotive Valve Gears.* Scranton, PA: International Textbook, 1928.

Hare, Jay V. *History of the Reading.* Philadelphia: John Henry Strock, 1966.

Harlow, Alvin F. *The Road of the Century.* New York: Creative Ave Press, 1947.

Holton, James L. *The Reading Railroad: History of a Coal Age Empire. Vol. I & II.* Laurys Station, PA: Garrigues House, 1992.

Hungerford, Edward. *Men of Erie.* New York: Random House, 1946.

Jones, Robert W. *Boston & Albany: The New York Central in New England, Vols. 1 & 2.* Los Angeles: Pine Tree Press, 1997.

Kiefer, P. W. *A Practical Evaluation of Railroad Motive Power.* New York: Steam Locomotive Research, 1948.

Kirkland, John, F. *Dawn of the Diesel Age.* Pasadena: Interurban Press, 1994.

Klein, Maury. *Union Pacific, Vols. I & II.* New York: Doubleday & Co., 1989.

Kratville, William, and Harold E. Ranks. *Motive Power of the Union Pacific.* Omaha, NE: Kratville Publishing, 1958.

Middleton, William D. *When the Steam Railroads Electrified.* Milwaukee, WI: Kalmbach Publishing,1974.

Morgan, David P. *Canadian Steam!* Milwaukee: Kalmbach Publishing, 1961.

———. *Locomotive 4501.* Milwaukee: Kalmbach Publishing, 1968.

———. *Steam's Finest Hour.* Milwaukee: Kalmbach Publishing, 1959.

Nowak, Ed. *Ed Nowak's New York Central.* Park Forest, IL: PTJ Publishing, 1983.

Pennsylvania Railroad. *1846–1896 Fiftieth Anniversary of the Incorporation of the Pennsylvania Railroad Company.* Philadelphia: Pennsylvania Railroad, 1896.

Ransome-Wallis, P. *World Railway Locomotives.* New York: Hawthorn Books Inc., 1959.

Reagan, H. C., Jr. *Locomotive Mechanism and Engineering.* New York: 1894.

Reck, Franklin M. *On Time.* Electro-Motive Division of General Motors. Lagrange, IL: Electro-Motive Division, 1948.

Rose, Joseph R. *American Wartime Transportation.* New York: Thomas Y. Crowell,1953.

Saunders, Richard, Jr. *Merging Lines: American Railroads 1900–1970.* DeKalb: Northern Illinois University, 2001.

———. *The Railroad Mergers and the Coming of Conrail.* Westport, CT: Greenwood-Heinemann Publishing, 1978.

Schafer, Mike and Brian Solomon. *Pennsylvania Railroad.* Minneapolis: Voyageur Press, 2009.

Shaughnessy, Jim. *Delaware & Hudson.* Berkeley: Howell North Books, 1967.

Shuster, Phillip, with Eugene L. Huddleston and Alvin F. Staufer. *C&O Power.* Carrollton, OH: Alvin F. Staufer, 1965.

Sinclair, Angus. *Development of the Locomotive Engine.* New York: Sinclair Publishing Company, 1907.

Smith, Warren L. *Berkshire Days on the Boston & Albany.* New York: Quadrant Press, 1982.

Solomon, Brian. *Alco Locomotives.* St. Paul, MN: Voyageur Press, 2009.

———. *The American Diesel Locomotive*. Osceola, WI: MBI Publishing, 2000.

———. *The American Steam Locomotive*. Osceola, WI: MBI Publishing 1998.

———. *Baldwin Locomotives*. Minneapolis: Voyageur Press, 2010.

———. *Burlington Northern Santa Fe Railway*. St. Paul, MN: Voyageur Press, 2005.

———. *CSX*. St. Paul, MN: Voyageur Press, 2005.

———. *Locomotive*. Osceola, WI: MBI Publishing, 2001.

———. *Railway Masterpieces: Celebrating the World's Greatest Trains, Stations and Feats of Engineering*. Iola, WI: Krause, 2002.

———. *Super Steam Locomotives*. Osceola, WI: MBI Publishing, 2000.

Solomon, Brian and Mike Schafer. *New York Central Railroad*. Osceola, WI: MBI Publishing, 1999.

Staufer, Alvin F. *Steam Power of the New York Central System, Volume 1*. Medina, OH: Alvin F. Staufer,1961.

———. *New York Central's Early Power 1831–1916*. Medina, OH: Alvin F. Staufer, 1967.

———. *Pennsy Power III*. Medina, OH: Alvin F. Staufer, 1993.

Staufer, Alvin F., and Edward L. May. *New York Central's Later Power 1910–1968*. Medina, OH: Alvin F. Staufer, 1981.

Steinbrenner, Richard T. *The American Locomotive Company—A Centennial Remembrance*. Warren, NJ: On Track Publishers, 2003.

Strapac, Joseph A. *Southern Pacific Review 1953–1985*. Huntington Beach, CA: Pacific Coast Chapter of the Railway and Locomotive Historical Society, 1986.

Swengel, Frank M. *The American Steam Locomotive: Volume 1, Evolution*. Davenport, IA: Midwest Rail Publishing, 1967.

Taber, Thomas Townsend, III. *The Delaware, Lackawanna & Western Railroad, Vols I & II*. Williamsport, PA: Lycoming Printing, 1980.

Vauclain, Samuel M. *Optimism*. Philadelphia: privately published, 1924.

Vauclain, Samuel M., with Earl Chapin May. *Steaming Up!* New York: Brewer & Warrren, 1930.

Walker, Mike. *Steam Powered Video's Comprehensive Railroad Atlas of North America—North East U.S.A.* Geaversham, Kent: Steam Powered Publishing, 1993.

Westing, Frederic. *Apex of the Atlantics*. Milwaukee: Kalmbach Publishing, 1963.

———. *The Locomotives that Baldwin Built*. Seattle: Superior Publishing, 1966.

White, John H., Jr. *A History of the American Locomotive*. Toronto: Dover Publications, 1968.

White, John H., Jr. *Early American Locomotives*. Toronto: Dover Publications, 1972.

Williams, Harold A. *The Western Maryland Railway Story*. Baltimore: Western Maryland Railway Company, 1952.

Winchester, Clarence. *Railway Wonders of the World, Volumes 1 & 2*. London: The Waverley Book Company Ltd., 1935.

Wiswessar, Edward H., P.E. *Steam Locomotives of the Reading and P&R Railroads*. Sykeville, MD: Greenberg Publishing Company, 1988.

Wright, Richard K. *Southern Pacific Daylight*. Thousand Oaks, CA: Wright Enterprises, 1970.

Brochures, Rulebooks, and Timetables

American Locomotive Company, *Louisiana Purchase Exposition*. New York City: 1904.

Baldwin Locomotive Works, *Exhibit at the Panama-Pacific International Exposition, San Francisco, Calif., 1915*. Philadelphia: 1915.

Baldwin Locomotive Works. *Triple Articulated Compound Locomotive for the Erie Railroad Company. Record No. 81*. Philadelphia: 1915.

Baldwin Locomotive Works. *The Fifty-Thousandth Locomotive. Record No. 92*. Philadelphia: 1918.

Baldwin Locomotive Works. *Eight-Coupled Locomotives for Freight Service. Record No. 99*. Philadelphia: 1920.

Boston & Albany Railroad, *Time-Table No. 174*. 1955.

Boston & Albany Railroad. *Facts about the Boston & Albany R.R.* 1933.

Central Vermont Railway. *Timetable 65, Northern and Southern Division*. 1965.

Conrail. *Pittsburgh Division, System Timetable No. 5*. 1997.

Delaware, Lackawanna & Western. *A Manual of the Delaware, Lackawanna & Western*. 1928.

Pennsylvania Railroad public timetables, 1942–1968.

New York Central System. *Rules for the Government of the Operating Department*. 1937.

New York Central System public timetables. 1943–1968.

Santa Fe public timetables. 1943–1964.

Southern Pacific Company. *Pacific System Time Table No. 17, Coast Division*. 1896.

Southern Pacific Company. Public timetables 1930–1958.

Southern Pacific. *Your Daylight Trip*. 1939.

Steamtown National Historic Site. *The Nation's Living Railroad Museum*. n.d.

Papers and Original Manuscripts

Clemensen, A. Berle. *Historic Reseach Study: Steamtown National Historic Site Pennsylvania*. US Department of the Interior. Denver: 1988.

Chappell, Gordon. "Flanged Wheels on Steel Rails—Cars of Steamtown" (unpublished).

Johnson, Ralph P., chief engineer. *The Four Cylinder Duplex Locomotive as Built for The Pennsylvania Railroad*. Presented in New York, May 1945. Published in Philadelphia.

Johnson, Ralph P., chief engineer. *Railroad Motive Power Trends*. Presented November 1945. Published in Philadelphia.

Meyer, C. W. *Comments on Ralph P. Johnson's Paper*, November 29, 1945. Presented November 1945. Published in Philadelphia.

Warner, Paul T. *The Story of the Baldwin Locomotive Works*. Philadelphia, 1935.

Periodicals

Baldwin Locomotives. Philadelphia (no longer published).

CTC Board. Ferndale, WA.

Jane's World Railways. London.

Modern Railways. Surrey, United Kingdom.

Official Guide to the Railways. New York.

Pacific RailNews. Waukesha, WI (no longer published).

Passenger Train Journal. Waukesha, WI (no longer published).

Railroad History, formerly *Railway and Locomotive Historical Society Bulletin*. Boston.

Railway and Locomotive Engineering (no longer published).

Railway Mechanical Engineer 1916–1952 (no longer published).

Railway Age. Chicago and New York.

TRAINS Magazine. Waukesha, WI.

Vintage Rails. Waukesha, WI (no longer published).

Index